For June -

The dearest of friends and travel companion

"Miss you loads"

FIRST TIME WE SAW PARIS

Or How a Small French Cafe Changed Our LIves

Neal Atherton
French Travel Writer

ALSO AVAILABLE

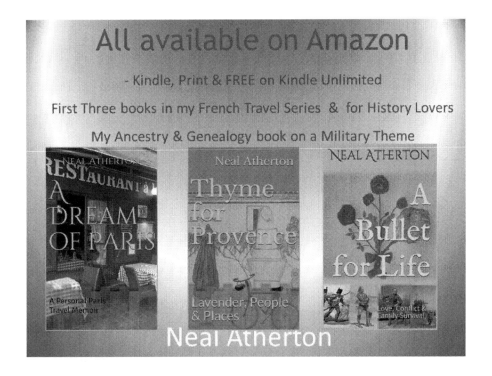

On Amazon Worldwide
SEARCH : NEAL ATHERTON

This is the first in a series of 4
Books on Travels in France

FOR A FREE SAMPLER OF ALL FOUR BOOKS Go To:

www.nealatherton.com/free

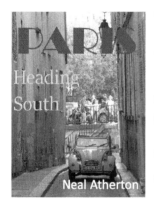

This one - The First Time We Saw Paris

Thyme in Provence - People and Places

Love of Paris over many visits to the French capital

Wine - visiting producers vineyards and cellars throughout France

INTRODUCTION TO OUR TRAVELS

W hat is my book about?

There have been so many books about buying and renovating a run-down property in France. A good number of books are written about buying a vineyard or an olive grove. Then there are more books about touring France in 2CV or horse and cart or even on foot. Or books about living in an ex-pat community.

What is it like though to briefly cross the channel and experience France and its people but sadly having to return to your 'normal' working life back home in England? Can you grow to love France and still feel immersed in its culture by taking fleeting visits for a couple of weeks, a few days or even a weekend?

I want to show you that you can do just that and inspire you to visit this amazing country.

This is not designed to be a guidebook but if you want to follow in my footsteps then you are very welcome. They go in a wonderful direction.

My wish though, is that you will discover your own treasured places and people and this book tells of the very beginnings of our love affair with French travel, a love that after a shaky start will develop throughout this series. It has been a remarkable ride for a reluctant traveller.

www.nealatherton.com/contact to register interest in Full French Travel Series.

Best regards and thank you for reading

Neal   Somerset   2019   www.nealatherton.com

FRENCH CATALONIA & MONSIEUR ARGENSON

W alking down a bakingly hot Rue Alsace Lorraine in Perpignan I was feeling very sorry for myself and rightly ex-tremely guilty about all that my family had endured now that their first French holiday had started so dreadfully badly.

All that will be revealed later.

On the right hand side of this narrow street we came across Le Malassis, a small typically French, Café bar, that shone out to our bedraggled party like the oasis of calm and welcome that we so desper-ately needed. For us this fine little café and its owner would become the turning point towards a lifelong love of France, its food, wine, culture and people. A small red metal table and four chairs was available on the narrow pavement terrace next to two young Japanese tourists sitting engrossed in their camera at the other occupied table. We were more than delighted to be seated at this table. The chef patron was leaning nonchalantly on the doorframe of the café taking a mid-morning cigarette break but keeping his chef's hat, his toque blanche, firmly on his head. My exposed and I suppose I have to admit it, a head that was rather now lacking in top cover was swiftly heading towards the colour of a London Bus or a glorious Languedoc Rosé wine. Monsieur Le Chef headed languidly over from his station at the door and looked pityingly at my once pale Lancashire complexion. He slowly took off his toque and placed it firmly on my head to protect me from the blazing sun.

Two words were all he said, 'Tete Rouge'.

Now France made sense, my mood transformed.
Yes, I was going to like this place, the café most certainly, but I would soon grow to love France as a travel destination and especially its people. From that moment on I always have. We will often return in years to come to Le Malassis and the delightful M. Argenson as we spent many happy times in his

delightful café with his generous warm hospitality right up until one day when we found Le Malassis shuttered up and closed. On our future visits to this small café we are remembered and greeted as friends rather than merely customers.

How did we get here and why?

Well it is a surprise to all of us because our family never ever took foreign holidays. Garlic butter! Well in our minds that surely was the least of the terrors that awaited the traveller that forsook the English resorts of Blackpool and Scarborough that really were quite far enough thank you as regards travel and the quest for excitement.

I still love Scarborough and am more than happy to revisit that magnificent North Sea coast but we did go to these two places rather often.

Mother just wanted to sit and enjoy being creative with her knitting while we three boys played pitch and putt golf or tennis very competitively as is the family tradition, or had potato chips or ice cream. That really was it for us as regards a travel education, we were all part of a cultural throwback to the traditional Lancashire Wakes weeks where everyone that lived and worked in the Lancashire Mill towns religiously went on holiday at the same time every year. There is available to view on-line a black and white film by future Oscar-winning director, John Schlesinger entitled 'Wakes Week' about the annual fixed holiday in Lancashire cotton towns and this film was shot in Blackburn. This short reel was filmed about 2 years before I became aware of being taken on this type of holiday that always started off from Blackburn train station but it gives an accurate reflection of how I recall these times and I also used to pull at the same metal drawers on the chocolate vending machine just as the boy does in the film, hoping a bar would fall out for free. You can find this film on the internet and it will give you a visual representation of the times that I have described.

Because 95% of the people of the town always went to the same holiday destination it was cheaper to go with the flow however boring it might become as the years went by. So as a family we always ended up on Blackburn train station waiting for the tired and dirty old steam excursion train to pull noisily but thrillingly onto the crowded platform, large letters and numerals strapped to the front of the engine denoting the destination. The train was always in this aged and dirty condition looking as if it was only ever given an outing to run a cheap holiday excursion and then be put back unloved into the engine shed to await another year. It would be fair to suppose that when I had my own family this conservative travel mentality did to a degree still remain in my DNA and indeed the Lancashire Wakes weeks as a ritual were still firmly in place at that time.

Our first exotic travel departure from the norm was when we somehow decided to have our honeymoon in Somerset, a very long way south for a Lancashire lad. I soon came to the realisation that if I could drive as far as Somerset and get back safely, even though on this first foray south I had to fix a breakdown on the way home, then I could even go to Devon or perhaps the far off county of Cornwall without a passport. So every year from then on that is what we started to do and thankfully my children grew up enjoying a far more expansive education of what England had to offer the determined traveller than I ever experienced when I was growing up. The great thing about still being in England was that obtaining and eating food was not a problem to me, for you must believe me that this practical aspect of travel was such a bonus to one whose most exotic encounter with olive oil was to have my mother buy it from the chemist so as to drip it into my ear to soften the wax.

We loved Devon and Cornwall and Niamh especially enjoyed the copious Cream Teas and we had so many ideal holidays in these southern counties even though it was around a six hour trip for us in a car that today would appear to be impossibly tiny. At my place of work I had the reputation of being the one person who every year would always get the best of holiday weather no matter the week I would chose to go. Early May, Mid-June, July school holidays or the old Lancashire September school break, it made absolutely no difference, without fail I would always be the gloating one that had once again booked the best possible weather. That shining red head of mine always returned to work glowing with health and there would always be the two weeks after returning that it took to peel the flaking skin off it to remind my jealous colleagues that once again they should have gone on holiday at the same time as me. The odds cannot be beaten. The curse for them is always cast.

Oh, but how that all dramatically changed one week in 1996.

We were staying quite near to the coastal town

of Looe in Cornwall and the first thing that was not spot-on about this holiday was that very unusually for me my unfailing knack of selecting excellent self-catering accommodation had inexplicably deserted me. This was a dog of a place. Definitely not a quaint fully equipped Cornish cottage but more a dwelling in the style of a rundown council house, very much like the one I had spent my childhood and teenage years in, although our house was not run down, well at least not on most days. However these basic conditions would still have been tolerable had it not been for one constant detail in that fateful week.

The weather.

This was very far from the fine sunny skies that I always have on holiday, the black heavy clouds rained down on us endlessly for fully five days from relentlessly unbroken Cornish skies. There was nothing to do to entertain ourselves or the children or if there was we had pretty much given up looking for it. In an act of sheer desperation we joined the National Trust. We did the deed at Cothele situated on the banks of the River Tamar, a fine house and looking around the inside of the property we enjoyed a very enjoyable and more importantly a dry visit. So the solid reasoning was that there must surely be other grand houses providing shelter to a party of wet Northeners and fortunately this proved to be the case. The children it has to be said were only moderately thrilled. To pull off the same stunt for next year's holiday might provoke a rebellion but as a couple we stayed members of the National Trust for 20 years until I fell out with them but that's another story.

So what was I to do? Deep into the long miserable Lancashire winter I was in urgent need of some fresh travel inspiration. Do I just take the easy way out and take a chance that 1996 was the year where I clearly had accidentally picked someone else's holiday slot and just put our weather misfortune down to that? Would my normally infallible long range weather forecasting skills return? Or more to the point, could I really afford to risk the wrath of two teenagers bored out of their minds being stranded in Cornwall on yet another wet week. On balance I could not.

I had never ever set foot in a travel agents shop, why would I? In those carefree pre-internet booking days all you had to do was browse the myriad of free holiday brochures that the poor postman had to carry to your door like a pack horse. Travel brochures that you had no qualms about requesting in bulk from the endless Sunday newspaper advertisements. Any modern day guilt about killing a rain forest had not yet entered into my consciousness back then. One quick phone call and then my immediate despatch of a Postal Order (I am old.) and the holiday cottage would be secured for the chosen week. I had never understood what those people were discussing in the travel agents in town. Who really needs them? It was only as I strolled through the streets, my mind just a little more open minded about holiday travel that I finally noticed that these places were actually mainly for people that holidayed abroad. As I didn't and never expected to do such an intrepid journey that simple fact had completely passed me by in the same manner the possibility of my going in a clothes shop unaccompanied had never crossed my mind also.

So feeling very courageous but desperately way out of my comfort zone I sheepishly approached the young lady sat at her desk with the world at her fingertips.

'France has good weather doesn't it?'

She agreed but didn't actually say 'not necessarily always though'.

'You want to go to France then?'

'Well possibly, but how do you do that?'

'You could fly'.

'Oh, I really don't think so. I have only just started driving the car on the motorway. Anyway, if the plane crashed then the family line comes to a sudden end'.

'Well if you are a bit unsure about flying then you could go by coach'.

'Coaches go that far.'

Anyway, of course I left her company with a brochure for coach holidays to the South of France. I never knew such a way of travel was possible. I mean how do you get a coach over that bit of water? I did have a sheltered life.

As a family we all mentally devoured the brochure that evening and found that there really was a whole new world out there but the actual idea of us doing something as different as this for a holiday was terrifying. Everybody else in the family was very keen but could I really finally leave the country and find something to eat as well? Or can I take my own food? Really the only feature in the brochure that I was scrupulously checking were the weather charts on the pages of each resort. They seemed to be guaranteeing certain weather for each individual week of the coming summer and that to me was very reassuring. All this meditation of mine was really an irrelevance as whatever my fears may have been, everyone else in the family had decided that they absolutely wanted to go to France and not just travelling a few miles beyond Calais but all the way right down to the Languedoc, a place called Canet Plage near Perpignan, close to the Spanish border.

The selected camp site of Le Brasilia looked like paradise to my sun starved family and in a moment of mad involuntary impulse I decided we were going to France. For the first time since my family ancestors were specifically created on the Banks of the River Darwen with the sole purpose to feed the East Lancashire cotton mills an Atherton would leave these shores without having the intention of invading the continent by force. I checked the brochure once more to substantiate the firm promise of great weather for a particular week and that was the holiday period that I settled on. We all agreed and decided that 10 days abroad would be enough, just to try it, a taster of a new strange land. The brochure did not actually mention Le vent Tramontane, the wind that mirrors the ferocious Mistral of Provence. There was a reason for that.

So then, next day it was back to the charming travel agent.

'We're going, definitely maybe. I have filled the booking form in but bear in mind you still have time to talk me out of it'.

'How do you want to pay?'

And so the deed was done. We were going to France. As I was to discover it's not quite that simple although the holiday booking and the paperwork were easily done.

Passports. We all needed passports. Wow, what items do we need for obtaining those. Well first of all a complicated form from the Post Office and then to crowd into a photo booth to have some hideous tiny photographs taken that surely would ensure we get stopped at customs.

Money. French francs and Travellers cheques. Where is the shop for that and why would any shop have French Francs in Lancashire? Well it turned out that they did and I felt very grown up and sophisticated explaining where we were travelling to. I made sure that we took enough money for emergency supplies like baked beans and tomato sauce and other Lancashire delicacies that I expected the English shops in France must supply. 'They do have English shops?'

Clothes. For everyone – even me. It is clear that we are certain to be far too hot in this promised wonderful land of perfect weather that the brochure displayed so deceitfully.

This is all good and fine but what about the actual logistics of making this journey. Each year I have been in the routine of simply throwing everything needed into the car, making sure the house is locked and off we go.

Where does this continental coach start its journey from?

Where does it stop en route and how do you survive 24 hour coach travel?

The worry list is endless but I as group leader really needed to show that I was in control of the situation and that I actually knew how to pull this feat off, so for me I immediately had to start a crash course of studying all about the trip and everything French. Well, I say crash course but in reality I probably studied for about six long months so I would know exactly what I was doing. Oh, and a course of French language tapes to learn the essentials while travelling to work in the car were a must. It may be that I will appear to be speaking French with a Lancashire accent but I was definitely going to order that meal in French and I was not going to be embarrassed in shops. Well, that was the plan anyway.

So, we just had to wait, suitcases packed, for this awful English winter to come to its end and we would then be off on our adventure. Although we did not know it at the time this new way of taking our holidays was going to change all our future travel plans and bring a tremendous enrichment to our lives and certainly a lot of fun along the way.

To the coach station then.

THE JOY OF COACH TRAVEL

N ow, the day dawned on what would be an experience that was surely a first for us. This was a long distance coach trip that would in fact take around 25 hours or so and would also be a journey that was undertaken virtually non-stop. Sure, I had in my youth often been on holiday to Blackpool or Scarborough by coach travel and I certainly recall without any affection the tedious trips to the Yorkshire coast even though they were in length only around four or five hours. So five times that length of journey appeared to be presenting quite a challenge. I would however come to learn that reassuringly there was at least in France an expectation that you would arrive somewhere as planned and would rarely be held up in traffic, embouteillages, unlike the way you are so often held up in solid traffic on the nightmare road that is the M6 in England.

Arriving in the early hours of the morning at the world famous architectural monument that is Preston coach station it immediately became clear that we had no idea at all as to where we actually had to go to board the coach. Another endearing feature you get as a bonus at that early hour is that you have to share the station with the local nightlife and from first appearances they certainly were unlikely to be of any help to us in our quest. We looked around the interior of this protectively listed (that means no one is allowed to make it better or preferably knock it down) concrete monstrosity, all the while making sure we avoided making any eye contact with our new neighbours and certainly hoped that we would not be offered a drink by them. Spotting two reasonably normal looking people with suitcases at the far end of the coach station we naturally assumed that they could only be here for the very same reason as ourselves unless they were supplying the additional early morning stimulants for the current station occupants. Sure enough we had located the correct spot for embarkation but the coach was late in arriving and that did not calm our nervousness at sharing the early morning space with drinkers who had either had a vat load of sustenance the night before or were just beginning to start early for the new day. The driver said he had stayed locally overnight so I could only assume he just couldn't have been bothered to get out of bed.

Now, coach travel is a strange mode of transport.

On a long distance coach you are sharing a space with people who are total strangers; these people are in turn total strangers to everyone else. For the alert coach traveller you will soon find that there are so many considerations and decisions that have to be made for your self-preservation. If you get them wrong then 24 hours on that coach will feel like a month, believe me. Should you get them right then it is a very enjoyable experience but you really must be mentally prepared to be much more outgoing socially than may be in the usual make-up of your character, you simply cannot just sit behind a book for all the length of that long journey, the time and space have to be shared but choose the occupiers of your space wisely.

Our feeder coach that departed from Preston heading for the South of England took forever to get there and on the coach the best game for you to while away the time is in trying to decide which passenger is ultimately going where after we all finally arrive at the coach exchange hub. I decided that anyone bedecked in shorts and football shirts was obviously going to Spain. The quieter ones, the fully dressed ones, were going to France. I was mostly correct in my snobbish generalisations. At the coach hub located just west of London it was the people in shorts that went off to stock up on beer and the quiet sensible ones, like us, just stood there seemingly bewildered as to what to do next. Fortunately there were plenty of women at the coach park, who actually appeared to be dressed as if they had just come back from being cast to play roles as staff extras in a film about British holiday camps. These women were scurrying frantically around trying to make sure that the multitude of coaches had the correct people on them, and I do mean that also in the true snobbish sense of the word. I was going abroad with the intention of enjoying the company around me but I also knew that I wanted some sleep and it looked for certain as if the other journey to Spain would not involve any break in drinking sessions. I generalise perhaps but I was secretly glad that I was not risking it on the Spanish coach.

First Rule of Coach Travel

Choose your seat carefully.

Now then, this means that an instantaneous assessment of the character of your fellow passengers is required - you have about one second to do this. Trained qualified psychiatrists cannot charge very much for one second but you really have to believe that you can do just as well as any trained professional who might for their appraisal require taking six months of weekly patient therapy. This evaluation is important as your happiness and wellbeing for the next 24 hours are dependent on getting this judgement correct.

Just as important as this is to make sure that you are seated nowhere near the on board toilet, 24 hours is a very long time if you get this wrong. Of course the bar is now freshly laden with alcohol and is located at the back of the coach and so if you are unlikely to be an around the clock drinker then do make sure you seat yourself well forward.

As you can tell a healthy dose of cynicism in

the nature of your fellow man is a requirement also. You must never though feel bad about discovering this latent character of yours as everyone else on the coach is carrying out exactly the same assessment with you. I might be the one more deserving of a harsh judgement than they are so no, I have no need to feel at all guilty. Oh, and by the way the truly crazy ones on your trip have always charged onto the coach to be the first to obtain the very front seats and the poor driver has absolutely no escape from the incessant inane chatter from these people. Having said all that, if you are unlucky enough to be conveyed by a driver that is under some misapprehension that he actually once had a career as some failed stand-up comedian then you have absolutely no escape from them as they have control of the microphone. That IS the time to get that book out.

Even then if you have managed to get all these opinions of your fellow travellers correct it is still not the right time to bond with them. That can come later. If you pick the wrong one then you will have them around you not just for the coach trip but for the entire holiday and if they manage to prise your address out of you during that time you may have these people for life. Again you have to understand that they are thinking exactly the same about you.

There are some chances on the early part of the trip to make a wise choice of companion and really you will eventually have to be friends with someone as this is definitely not a holiday for 'Billy no mates'. The first real opportunity presents itself at the first toilet break stop. Perhaps you could give out your first brief words in the Gents loo, if you are a man of course. Just see how it goes. Maybe you could make an observation that the water is really hot from the taps or how you just hate those hand dryers. Being English then probably the state of the weather will make up the first contact words of choice. You can learn a lot though in this brief encounter.

Outside into the fresh air you once again will see the gaggle of smokers in the party. That either draws you in to their circle or if you are a firmly committed non-smoker they are suitably placed in a total exclusion zone in your mind. Whichever way that situation may resolve itself in your character assessment then the choice of potential companion available to you will now be considerably reduced. So do you now tentatively fix on someone to see how you are suited to socialise around them during the next 10 days? Rather like a lion picking off that gazelle at the back of the pack.

Of course you can wait until you are all on the ferry and that will provide you with plenty of people watching time but the moment must surely come when you are compelled to make meaningful and decisive conversation. Unfortunately I am afraid all this works in reverse and you may have been picked off already and your fate is sealed. So don't leave it too long - this is fun.

For me as a first time tourist heading on a journey abroad the final English section of the journey when the coach heads down into Dover harbour is quite a thrill, catching sight of the ferries in the passenger docks makes this adventure all seem very real. This approach into Dover is quite a mundane event now for us and probably will be for most of you reading this but even now I still get a sense of how exciting it was on that first time and I trust that you can also cast your memory back in the same way.

Our coach pulls in to Dover docks just in time to see the shorts and football shirt people getting back onto their coach heavily laden with fresh liquid supplies. We potential French tourists though are such a civilized bunch of English ambassadors, so of course we scoff at their caricature display of the Englishman abroad and we content ourselves with a cup of tea. However true terrors await us so something stronger might have helped, this is a situation that has never happened to us before, not even in Cornwall – it is the time to go through customs.

Truly, if there is anyone that can make you feel guilty until proved innocent it is Her Majesty's customs officers. Why is this? I certainly have nothing to hide and even my passport photo could be a likeness of me if they look closely enough. I am afraid though that even 20 years on they always do make me feel this way and you just know that there is a strong possibility that you will confess to something, anything really. Perhaps it will be that cheating you did early on in life at school as a 7 year old and will cause you to be left stranded at Dover or worse.

Well, what have I got to be worried about?

At least I have my passport with me and that is more than can be said about the poor man sitting about three seats behind me. He is completely terror struck at this minor omission from his packing and the entire colour has been drained from his face. Now the location of our passports was the most important object that I fastidiously checked to be on my person at least twenty times before leaving home and then even on the coach after leaving Preston bus station I reviewed the contents of my bag at least once an hour. I will continue to do that for the rest of this holiday as well and probably not change this nervous habit for the rest of my life when travelling abroad. Sadly, no matter where this poor guy looks in his bags or his pockets his passport is definitely not with him on the coach and he admits that he does know for certain that it is not with him because he recalls that he has indeed left it behind, he can visualise this vital document lying there on the dining table back at home.

Anyway the British are nothing if not resourceful and the Holiday Camp ladies instantly hatch a cunning plan. How sensible this plan actually is I am not so sure but it swings into seamless operation.

I must place on record here that I took absolutely no part in this.

The passport less man is hidden down on the floor of the coach between the seats and a fellow traveller brought from the bar area at the rear to occupy his actual seat to endeavour to avoid any suspicion. The customs men have asked the driver to ensure that all passports are waved in the air as they make their way down the coach. What they neglected to add about this operation was that they were bringing their cuddly pet dogs onto the coach with them. Somehow it seems likely that anyone on the floor may end up suffering more than a nip to the ankles. The game is surely up for this absurd scenario but the men in blue seem initially content that passports are in good supply but then they start making their way down the coach due to their dogs either needing a toilet break or the canine minds have become suspicious about something.

Suspicious - indeed they are.

A young man's back pack has attracted their nosey attentions and before they can get as far down the coach as the prostrate man bereft of his passport they whisk the young man off with the dogs smiling and yapping behind him and I am certain that he is left ruing the fact that he did not buy his 'supplies' in France. What it does do however is make the customs men happy enough not to bother to return and the coach and the rest of us are sent on our way including the extremely relieved man sans passport. Fortunately for his current nervous state no one has mentioned that if he gets caught without paperwork coming back the other way the consequences are likely to be far worse for him. Like Napoleon he could end his days in solitary exile by the French. Still, he feels he has enough money for the duration of the trip and his misplaced confidence in being able to handle customs is now at such a peak that he feels nothing else can go wrong.

The loading of vehicles onto the ferry begins and once again for us this is a totally new experience. Our coach makes its way hesitantly up the winding ramp from the quayside to the ferry and is then swallowed up into the mouth of this cavernous beast. You try as soon as you can to make a mental note of the deck and door numbers that you are going to require to find the coach again when disembarking in Calais. In hindsight a written note would have been an even better idea. Clearly being the idiot responsible for any delay at the other side of the channel would make you very unpopular with other travellers.

When you enter into the passenger decks of such a large vessel you quickly lose any sense of where you actually are on the ship and this makes the disembarking at the other side liable to descend into a bit of a panic. That prophecy is for later.

Once on the ferry the situation that now presents itself is that you have an opportunity to size up your fellow passengers again and basically look around the party for a friendly face. An obstacle to this is the curiously English type of behaviour displayed by quite a number of the passengers and that is the desire to head straight to the bar. In some ways this can be a benefit for you because if propping up the bar is not your style it does narrow down the field of potential 'friends' considerably. The shorts and football shirt crowd win the race to the bar comfortably but you also disappointingly see some from your French bound coach desperately fighting their way to the front so obviously suffering from a severe midday alcohol deficiency and needing a prescription urgently. These, we and other passengers will discount from the list of those we want to spend the next 10 days together as close companions. Probably it is that we just don't have such a need for alcohol at all times of the day but maybe it is just that we are not prepared to keep buying a round of drinks every hour on holiday, our French francs only stretching so far of course. Others from the coach are frantically trying to order a full English breakfast even though it is after noon and that prompts you to mentally discount these as holiday friends also as it is most unlikely that they are going to want to immerse themselves in French culture. It is tough work making new friends. I have probably in my mind already ruled out 80 % of my fellow man on the coach and I begin to wonder if we are also ruled out due to our obvious determination not to be classed as the 'Englishman abroad'. Certainly nobody as far as I can tell has so far tried to make friends with me but that might just be because I am clearly lost in another world with all my people watching and filling my mental notebook.

Soon though the die is cast on this trip and what a joy this will be for us as we make new friends. This was mutual and so much the better for it. We got chatting to a lovely family with similar age children and we all got on famously. Did they choose us? I like to think so because I do feel that I have become such a snob with this people watching that I probably don't really deserve anyone being friendly so I am more than happy that someone has seen through this aloofness and thought in Lancastrian terms that 'hees probly all reight'. Actually, that's unlikely as they are Welsh and don't understand the Lancashire dialect. However, this companionship will all end in tears at the end of the week, mainly happy ones, except that is for our daughter who is going to have one of her first teenage heartbreaks with one of our attractive new friends.

Standing outside on the upper deck of the ferry you find that even in early summer it is quite a bracing experience, quite cold but exhilarating. I want to stay on deck longer than Niamh does as she is getting quite chilled and she goes back inside. The English Channel is a very interesting shipping lane and vessels appear likely to pass very close to our ferry as it makes the way through fairly choppy seas on a straight course across to Calais. These vessels don't hit us of course but you are close enough to be able to speculate on the destination of these ships, large and small, many displaying that they are from countries very far away from these waters, currently heading to ports around the English coast bringing vast cargos to add to the British national debt.

Never having done a sea trip before I find it is exciting and puzzling, in fact the most boating of any kind that I have done is on Lytham St Anne's Fairhaven Lake in Lancashire as a child. I thought even that was a bit over stimulating to be honest. The puzzling part of this for me as I stand on deck is that we seem to be heading straight for the French coastline; a part of land that even I can tell does not have a port. The exciting part is just in actually seeing the French coast for the very first time, for us this really is exotic. I would imagine that you had the same feeling the very first time you made this journey or left your home country as a new traveller. All I can make out on the shoreline are some French dog walkers, well the walkers are probably French and come to think of it the dogs will be as well. Sorry do let me go on. There are definitely no sunbathers though but I still live in hope the brochure was correct about the weather forecast.

Where then is the port of Calais?

Are we going to go ashore on some sort of landing craft, straight onto the beach and then be accosted by French customs officers scurrying from the sand dunes? No we are not, for as close as the ferry is to the shore we are not going to land on the beach. We start a slow heavy turn to the left (what is left in nautical terms?) and this eventually takes us parallel to the coast and we can do some more people watching as we look towards the sands and that gives us a snapshot of French beach life. As we turn it is difficult to see straight ahead very clearly but soon you can unmistakably make out the Calais harbour entrance but more especially Le Beffroi de l'Hotel de Ville. The tower on the horizon is quite a distinctive structure and one that as the years progress has become our landmark welcoming us to France and the beginning of our adventures.

◆ ◆ ◆

We are here. We are in France.

This I am afraid for us is where the fun really starts and I have not in any way studied this ritual of disembarking, I probably thought we just stayed on the coach all the way across. Obviously not. We have now to find our coach again. Yes, I know you are thinking that a coach is quite large and that it is probably a bit careless to lose one in a confined space but lose it we have. First of all we can't even find the stairs that we had previously used to come up to the deck and believe me I had thought when coming up initially to the exit onto the passenger deck that these stairs were pretty large and unmissable as well.

We ultimately find some stairs that look vaguely familiar and anyhow we are basically swept down these stairs in the crush of people heading back to their vehicles. It very much reminds me, unfortunately you have to be British to get this, of leaving a soccer ground as a youngster in the days before these were turned into all seater stadiums, back then occasionally having the experience of actually going out from the stadium to the street with my feet off the ground, my body squeezed and trapped, being carried along between the throngs. Here also we have no other choice but to go with the flow of people and use these stairs and quite unsurprisingly our coach is not where we left it. Quelle surprise.

Wrong stairs of course, but clearly we cannot go back up them to try to get our bearings from the starting point and this ferry is so cavernous that our coach could be anywhere, it might not even be on this deck. The feeling of being lost and possibly stranded is dreadful, it is a real sick to the stomach feeling. We genuinely have no idea where to start looking. I don't even know which way the ship is facing. Looking around me for some familiar faces, friends or mere fellow travellers, I see none. No doubt they are not as stupid as me and are already on the coach. This is definitely a more serious proposition than forgetting where you left your car on the supermarket car park. The sinking feeling gets worse when people start switching on their car engines as you just know those big containing doors are going to open soon, very soon. I send our son one way and I go the other but I cannot see anything resembling our coach. Then I hear a cry from James on the other side of the bulkhead and he has spotted our coach some distance farther down the hold on the opposite side of the stairs we had emerged from. Looking for sure like a bunch of crazy, desperate and bedraggled idiots we edge our way between ever so many parked vehicles hoping that they have no intention of moving. If we don't make it soon however there is a real danger we will be asphyxiated. I am not feeling a very proud group leader just at that moment in time.

We eventually get to the coach, our holiday camp uniformed organiser giving a very long hard stare at me. She knows it is my fault, not the others in the family. We, well should I say I, slink onto the coach, head firmly bowed. I can think what I like about everyone else in our coach party after my interminable people watching but one thing is absolutely clear – NO ONE wants to be my friend, not even for a round of drinks.

FIRST TIME I
SAW PARIS

O K, I know this probably sounds naïve now as we all know Paris I suppose. Today, twenty or so years on from my first visit so do I after so many wonderful days spent in the city during those intervening years but even now the ap-proach into Paris whether it is made by road or Eurostar still has a particular thrill for me. It certainly did on that balmy early summer evening back in 1997. It was a real event in our lives for us and one that I still recall quite vividly with a special feeling. The first time I saw Paris was truly very exciting – I hope it was for you. Never let that feeling leave you and it will repay you well on every visit you make.

This account is of that first trip but the full story of our relationship with Paris must be for another time, another book. Writing chronologically cannot always work and Paris is special to me and those thoughts and recollections I will eventually put altogether in one story, for my pleasure certainly and hopefully yours also.

Coming in to Paris on the Autoroute the blue distance Kilometre signs some of which have period lettering remind you of the art deco times between the wars. The kilometres on these markers gradually reduce in value and you find yourselves in the Paris suburbs. On this first visit we get a great view of the new Stade de France coming to completion in time for the soccer World Cup being hosted by France in 1998. France won but we missed that party. The Charles de Gaulle airport is adjacent to the road and the coach seems to try to keep pace with the taxiing aircraft but these win and you have an excellent view of them becoming airborne. Once in the suburbs these neighbourhoods are nothing special to view and in fact appear quite neglected and intimidating. The graffiti is everywhere, no solitary space is left untouched and you find yourself open mouthed at the resourcefulness of the street artist at work in the dead of night, perilously risking his or her life for their art.

Soon you can get a sense of what the city of Paris promises to the visitor.

Looking over to the hill of Montmartre the Sacre Coeur Basilica reflects its light back out over the city and you begin to try to visualize how the village of Montmartre may have appeared in the Belle Epoque when the many artists lived and worked in its rambling streets. The reality of Montmartre today is quite different to the days of the impressionist painters but this is what Paris will always do to you, she makes you imagine. You are provided with virtual reality images in your mind. Turning back to look the other way over the cityscape you are dazzled by the many vast neon signs that are blindingly bright and colourful, fixed to the high rise buildings and advertising in typically French script anything from cars and air travel to restaurants. You can sense the excitement that awaits you as a first time visitor to this vibrant city. Sensibly you do have to remind yourself that this is only going to be a fleeting visit and this is not the main purpose of your journey but that fact just heightens your feelings as you approach the city determined to squeeze every last drop of pleasure from this special part of the trip.

This city will not disappoint us on this introduction to it and this brief experience opens the road to many more visits for us solely to enjoy Paris and all that it can offer to this lover of history, food and wine. Oh, I knew about the history part before we set off on our journey - but the food and wine. Oh, what a discovery they would be. My only previous taste of the exotic was indeed garlic bread and that would all have to thoroughly change and most enjoyably so. We will only be here to admire central Paris for a couple of hours or so but the impression it makes on us in this short time changes our future travels forever. We will always incorporate Paris into our French jaunts as often as we possibly can and it will be a future venue for the most memorable times with friends and family and hopefully with still many more excursions to come.

We soon leave the suburbs behind and we are at the Place de l'Etoile or Place Charles de Gaulle with the instantly recognisable Arc de Triomphe at its centre. This is a stunning first view of the famous centre of Paris with the Arc de Triomphe brightly lit up against the backdrop of the clear Paris night and then seeing spread out in front of this giant edifice the nearly two kilometre length of the Avenue des Champs Elysees with streaks of light from the cars all down the centre and the boulevard being illuminated from either side by cafés and bars and vivid exclusive shop fronts.

First of all however this Place must be crossed and certainly not on foot but from the safety of a seat in the coach. The driver very hesitantly inches his way to the starting line waiting for that smallest of gaps that heralds the starting gun. I change my gaze away from the exciting new sites all around me and look down from my high vantage point at the bewildering road below and see that barely two feet from the side of the coach and immediately below my window is a Citroen automobile with its manic driver, hunched over the steering wheel, hustling for a way forwards. He has positioned his vehicle exactly at a 90 degree angle to the side of the coach. All around our coach there are cars cutting in at speed into any possible space but somehow it seems that no one crashes into another as they insert their vehicle into an opening that only they can judge. Apparently it must be that the story claiming that your insurance is not valid on the Place de l'etoile concentrates the mind. Surely though I would consider that just being in your car on this frenzied spot could induce a panic attack thus making a helpless driver become rigid and immobilised in the centre of this impossible roundabout. Our coach though is still somehow moving forward, the speedometer barely registering, and we edge our way over without any scrapes to the exit leading onto the Champs Elysees. A very definite mental note is made that any thought of taking my own vehicle into the centre of Paris is not to be acted on – not ever.

The splendid avenue Champs Elysees is just amazing to experience just in taking in its length alone but most of all in observing the vibrancy of its street life and there is no better time to see it than on a clear balmy night when it is crowded with people strolling and eating and drinking at the many terrace cafés. Watching the people on the pavements you notice the flower seller proffering a single stem into the hands of a pretty young lady. She gratefully accepts and her partner soon realises it is not an admiring gesture – he has to pay for it. The whole scene I might add is especially pleasing from the comfort of a coach.

What would you say is the most famous feature that you can recall about the Champs Elysees that now suddenly you find is really there stretching out in front of you?

Is it Le Fouquets Restaurant at 99 Champs Elysees with its famous red exterior, the tables comfortingly secluded behind the neat hedges around the terrace? I remember reading a book by the English writer Frank Muir who described how in the weeks just after the war he drove in uniform over to Paris from England in his open topped sports car pulling up right outside Le Fouquets and in those different times was actually able to park his car and leave it there. He relates how he was able to be enjoying a delightful meal in the days following the liberation that contrasted with the frugal situation back at home. It is so evocative to see the famous old restaurant bustling with many stylish contented diners no doubt with loud chatter over a superb long meal and a bottle or two of wine.

Or for you is it located just over the road, the famous white M sign for McDonalds? This is the only white sign of that famous chain of restaurants for it was demanded of them for the privilege of being on such an exclusive venue. The children certainly think that this is the highlight but they cannot this evening stop for a 'happy meal'.

The men on the coach are purring at the glass fronted exclusive car showrooms, amazing to see on such a boulevard of shops and cafés.

Perhaps it could be Maison Laduree with its exquisite shop front that reminds you of sophisticated times past, displaying their perfect macarons in all their colourful glory?

For the ladies in our party the real highlight, though not necessarily on this visit but most certainly in years to come would have to be the large Sephora Perfume store. This fragrance store is still open at this late hour and as we pass tantalizingly by you can see that from the entrance there leads a long gently sloping ramp that makes it appear as if you may be going into a stadium, which I suppose to a certain degree you are. Along both sides of this ramp there are a multitude of glamourous store assistants, male and female, poised and ready to squirt you with any number of delicate scents. After negotiating that first runway you then emerge into this cavernous apparently underground space where you will be made aware that if they have not got your favourite perfume, lotion, eau de cologne etc… then it doesn't exist. It is a store that would test the limit on my credit cards in years to come and those of many of our friends. Not tonight however.

The list could go on and in our future visits to Paris we will happily stroll down both sides of the avenue and that is the only real way to gain full appreciation of this most famous and beloved of avenues. Yes, we also did it in the Paris rain.

When the coach finally reaches the end of the Champs Elysees, it is the sight of this particular location that really captures my imagination. For the first time in my life I am on the Place de la Concorde, the largest and most famous square in all of Paris. On being there it evokes any amount of remembrances from your knowledge of it and in your imagination. It is the site of the most infamous events of the French Revolution, scene of the execution of Louis XV and Marie Antionette amongst hundreds of other lesser luminaries.

My interest is in the more recent history of Paris so in my mind I can visualise the fighting in this Place towards the end of the war as Paris is finally liberated in August 1944. The square was then most certainly not a place to find yourself in as the cornered Germans were harassed and shot down as they vacated the Hotel Meurice and their other occupied headquarters of Central Paris, their occupation signposts in Germanic script ready to be torn down. How this Place makes your mind race as you take in the entire scene around you.

At last, the coach comes to a halt adjacent to the fountains facing down towards the Tuilleries Gardens that are now firmly in darkness and at this time of night looking uninviting. These Gardens would for us become one of our most favourite spots in France, but that will be for another future day. Towering up in front of us as we step from the coach is the giant Egyptian obelisk brightly decorated in hieroglyphics that glorifies the reign of the Pharaoh Ramesses II, a treasure originally located in Luxor and given over to France in the 19th Century. A truly fabulous monument.

Once outside on the Place we can examine at close hand some objects and sites that we have only seen previously in books and photos. That surely has to be the great joy of travel, to see such familiar yet never seen before objects and places. What we are seeing on this first evening I am certain will be for many people reading this just familiar and routine but just like any place or object seen for the very first time there is no naivety here on this night but only wonder. These sights and sounds I am happy to say will never appear as mundane but will still give a thrill for us to see over and over again. Certainly the children are in wonderment and I have to admit so am I. However, I do sadly totally despair at the sight of the odd one or two of my fellow travellers who simply view this majestic place as just another cigarette break and the only fleeting pleasure they are interested in is lit up between their lips. There is no point wasting any informative lecture on the wondrous sights obliviously shining down on them far more brightly than any cigarette.

Much too soon we are ushered back on to the coach but this is not to be for very long. Crossing the Pont de la Concorde it is to the left that we catch sight downriver of Notre Dame, the historic Cathedral that is all splendidly lit up on the evening skyline of the islands. As the coach speeds away across the river we just have time to take in this section of the River Seine from its banks, night-time reflections of the bustling cafés and restaurants that sit alongside the water shining back at us from the shimmering river. Now it is time for us to catch sight of the truly recognizable sight that signifies Paris and a 'wow' comes not just from the mouths of the children but also from most of the adults as Gustave

Eiffel's most famous and crazy creation comes into our view. The famous tower is a structure that was conceived as a temporary exhibit for the 1889 Paris World Fair but is of course still here dominating the Paris skyline. All brightly lit up now and very soon the tower will be sparkling and twinkling in the clear night sky, the sight of this monument is a fabulous and unforgettable first viewing. We get out of the coach and are able to sit at the top of the Champs de Mars, joining in with countless others reclining on the dry grass as they come to the end of an evening's picnic (with wine), the temperature is still pleasantly warm and we gaze in wonder at this structure and all present agree it is breathtakingly impressive to see this in reality and not merely in photographs or film. Thankfully, once again that initial wonder for us will be retained for future visits.

Our children are so excited at this view that they make many attempts to record this spectacular photo opportunity shining in front of their eyes. Sadly, in those pre digital camera days I am afraid they will be rather unsuccessful but it will be two more weeks before we eventually find only grainy unfocused images emerging from the exposed reel of film. Camera technology has advanced so much now that even from the tiny camera on our phone we can expect a quality souvenir ready for immediate posting to our friends on Instagram. So, frustratingly it must be that we live on our memories this first time around.

The radiant looming Tower draws you in and quite a few from our coach, ourselves included, move closer to it down the Champs de Mars approach but it is unfortunately the catchphrase of Marty Feldman from that incredibly funny 'Lightning Tours' sketch from the late 60's that gets us scurrying in reverse.

'Everybody back on the coach.'

Then a chorus of 'Wait for me'.

It does feels like a lightning tour and indeed it is but perhaps no bad thing for that as it really whets the appetite for a return trip although I think not for the smokers who apparently are merely content to smoke anywhere and have seen nothing to interest them further.

On y va, off we go, there are many more delights to see but there are more grumblings on the coach that someone had wasted most of a lighted cigarette having tried to cram a whole packet worth of smokes into a 15 minute stop.

◆ ◆ ◆

The difficulty and certainly regret that comes with writing in hindsight is surely that at the time of experiencing your travel have no conception about the future. If you possibly had such a gift then you would not only be able to let your imagination run wild about past events in Paris but you would be able to realize that the places you are now seeing on this night would shortly become more famous and would be marked indelibly in history. Tragically, some of these views would be historic in a very short space of time. One of these places the coach is crossing over now, the Pont de l'Alma. This evening in June 1997 it stands as a merely commemoratively important bridge recalling the Battle of Alma in the Crimean war of 1854 where a rare Franco/British collaboration brought them victory.

In just two short months Princess Diana would meet with tragedy in the adjacent Alma Tunnel but a thought of such appalling magnitude could not even be speculated about on this night. We would as a family a couple of years later travel back to Paris by Eurostar and my French by then was sufficiently good enough to decipher a metro announcement that indicated that it would be in our interest to leave the train at the next station and change routes. This next stop turned out to be the Pont de l'Alma station. Emerging from the platform below the first sight for us was the Flame of Liberty statue completely encased with tributes, mainly floral, but of every possible type and significance to the person that was using this spot as a place to be remembering Princess Diana. It was quite a poignant sight and especially as I reflected that we had passed by that very spot so very shortly before that dreadfully sad historic event.

The coach then takes us across the river, with the quays of the Seine dotted at intervals with strolling couples, contentedly returning home after a meal in one of the many cafés and restaurants lining the river bank and adjacent side streets. The coach driver is good enough to take us on a short detour and he turns left off the Rue Rivoli into the Place Vendome. Looking back over twenty years later it is with hindsight that this would not just have been an opportunity to simply see this exclusive square filled with luxurious shops, especially many famous Parisian jewellers such as Boucheron, Jaubalet and Van Cleefs and Arpels, for most of us our wallet size making this just delightfully pleasing window shopping.

As the entire world now knows it was here in a few weeks' time from our evening visit that this Place would be the starting point of the tragic drama to be played out surrounding the last moments of Princess Diana. Tonight it is a dazzling scene of ostentatious luxury with the most expensively grand automobiles turning into the entrance way of the Ritz Hotel with no hint of the historic events to shortly come in late August 1997.

Looking out of my window I can sense a sniff of disdain from these beautiful people as they emerge from their opulent cars and catch sight of our coach, all of our eyes turned to be looking into this sumptuous goldfish bowl. The driver senses the mood as well and takes his leave of this splendid square.

As we retrace our steps so as to turn right onto the Rue Rivoli again there is another opportunity for me to let my imagination add colour to the scene. I can visualize the ranks of German soldiers parading at this very spot from the photographs from the dark period of the Paris occupation. Looking left down towards the Louvre I can remember that brilliant photo by Robert Doiseneau of the line of young school children, arms linked together crossing the road with their schoolteacher, all traffic stopped but poised to speed away. Paris is full of such locations that have been captured at an historical moment or simply an everyday scene caught by the camera of a great photographer. If you are coming to Paris then check out the work of Doiseneau and his photographs will enrich your experience of the visit immensely.

In my mind and having lived a sheltered life back home in Lancashire there was one restaurant that I always assumed was the most famous one in the world. This was the art nouveau decorated Maxims, a restaurant that seemed to symbolise everything you had heard and read about Paris and its portrayal of glamour and celebrity. All those thoughts are most certainly true but even I should have realized that Paris is full of great world class restaurants and coming to the end of the 20th Century Maxims has serious competition. The coach turns into Rue Royale and there at No:3 is Maxims in all its Belle

Epoque splendour - fabulous. The restaurant appears as we peer out from the coach window to be so exclusive that I feel that if a Lancastrian peasant such as myself should even dare to approach the door then he would be moved swiftly to the gutter. My restaurant dining confidence would certainly grow over the years but I still have not eaten at Maxims.

Woody Allen had not at that time made his wonderfully evocative film 'Midnight in Paris' but you may recall the scene when the two characters time travel to revisit La Belle Epoque at Maxims and that for me sums up how I felt at seeing such a Paris foodie monument for the first time. My imagination was already with them in that yet to be filmed scene.

I really want to stop, go to a restaurant, sit at an outdoor table, stay the night, stay a week but it cannot be on this first fleeting sight of the French capital.

The coach carries on up towards Place Madeleine and onwards past the Opera House just in time to see that evenings audience drifting down the front steps and into the Paris night, no doubt for a late meal or simply a glass of wine on a sidewalk table. So we are soon moving onto the Peripherique, and very scary that is too, leading on to the Autoroute and the

South and the promised sunshine beckons.

NIGHT TRAVEL TO THE SOUTH

The journey on down the Autoroute from Paris is made during the pitch dark night and night travel on a coach is quite an experience and for us a new one. There is something strangely comforting about traveling in the quiet of the night as the coach had in a sense sort of shut down as regards any noise or chatter or movement of passengers but also you have a slight sense of danger as you want desperately to try to wander off to sleep but fear that the driver will not stay awake. To achieve an almost non-stop service for 24 hours the two drivers drive the coach for around four hours or so and if they wish they can at the end of their shift retire to a small coffin like compartment located under the floor at the front of the coach but accessed from the outside. If you are the sort of person that was in any way suffering from claustrophobia you could never do this job. The very thought of being sealed in a container that is part of a missile travelling at 70 miles per hour is terrifying. They do though somehow seem to actually manage to get some sleep but as the 24 hours progress they start to look decidedly the worse for wear and a long shower at the final destination must be something for them and the adjacent passengers to expectantly look forward to.

It is very shortly after joining the autoroute south of Paris, l'autoroute du Soleil, that the coach slows to a halt. We had come up to the scene of a very recent accident involving a large German tourist coach, one of those that has a large box trailer behind it used for carrying all the additional luggage. This unfortunate coach appeared to have been hit from behind by a large truck and then been forced off the road into a ditch. There were many young people wandering around the edge of the autoroute looking a little dazed and shocked. The most obvious consequence of this accident was that the luggage container trailer had been totally split open and all its contents were splayed everywhere around the scene with hundreds of personal belongings littering the road, the ditch and the banking to the side of the autoroute. Fortunately it appeared that the only serious casualty of the accident was the luggage trailer and the rear of the coach and although obviously shaken up the occupants were to all intents OK.

We had arrived at the accident at the same time as the Police and Fire Service, Le Sapeurs Pompiers, and they quickly and with purpose set about working on the scene before them. Now, I don't know if you have ever driven in England but you may be aware of how an accident on the Motorway in Britain is dealt with by the emergency services. It is not as here in France, not at all. What appears to happen in the UK, I generalize of course but not much, is that if say two small cars collide and slightly block one lane out of three available then the Police and Fire Brigade and probably a couple of ambulances will arrive and at that point the whole motorway will be blocked. They will take care to establish that the occupants have suffered no more than a broken fingernail, taking around an hour to do so and then try to determine the exact cause of the crash from a hundred different angles despite the ultimate insurance claim to anyone involved being only a tiny fraction of the cost of having all this attention from the

Emergency Services thrown at the scene.

Only when all is logged and cleared to the satisfaction of all concerned will the by now miles of stationery traffic be allowed to file past the minor collision. Your journey having had a couple of hours added to it because some idiot ran into the back of another vehicle causing minimal damage. As I say I exaggerate just a tiny bit.

That scenario does not happen here. Not even close. Yes, they establish people are OK but after that the main focus of the action takes place in clearing the road of any debris and belongings. Any vehicle involved in the accident is moved immediately off the road and the lanes are clear to go. This takes around 5 or 10 minutes at most and to us this accident has appeared to be quite a major collision. They seem uninterested as to who is at fault, their only concern is to scoop everything out of the way and let the traffic go on its way. I could not imagine a greater contrast with what we see at home. Another early French lesson.

We are very soon moving on our way once again and travel on through the night, possibly sleeping a little but it is one of those types of sleep you experience when you are never actually sure if you nodded off at all or just had your eyes closed and really hoped to drop off to sleep. I must actually have slept a little because I awoke as I felt the coach come to a halt and our coach attendants were moving outside quietly at the front of the coach with the driver. It is a really strange feeling of being half awake in the dead of night and by now feeling like you had been on this coach for many days without sleep. We find ourselves in Macon, Burgundy. This is the diesel filling stop that all coach and truck drivers use when heading to the South of France and it is rather like a large trucker's stop with oversized petrol pumps and a refreshment service area that is clearly still very busy with long distance drivers even at 3 am.

One or two of us also get off to use the facilities but we are made to feel like aliens from another planet as we make our way past the truckers in the café who are eating substantial meals and seem to be enjoying decent quantities of rough red wine as well. Eventually the coach is refilled with fuel and you can I assume imagine what had to be done with the on-board toilet. All the passengers are accounted for and we drive on. The autoroute at this time of night is very quiet and nothing at all now slows our progress to the South. The pair of drivers had swapped over again and the driver from Paris has retreated to his little claustrophobic pod hoping for some rest. We journey on until we take note that the sun starts to appear on the horizon. On to Montelimar, the home of nougat.

The coach stops here for a while at the Montelimar services where I am sure that there is food but all you can see here initially are masses and masses of nougat both in packets and in giant slabs. If you were not aware before stopping here that Montelimar is the nougat capital of France then you will do now. I am sorry but nougat is not one of my faves and to be honest at this time of day I really want breakfast not something sweet but even at this early hour they are doing a roaring trade with this sweet confection in its multitude of colourful sticky varieties.

I have certainly noticed the nougat but another thing I definitely noticed when crossing from the coach to the service area is that the weather is very bitterly cold. It is also extremely windy. Now correct me if I am wrong but did the travel brochure or the travel agent make mention that this state of affairs could be a possibility. They most assuredly did not. They promised me warmth and wall to wall sunshine. They did not at any time say that you would find it to be colder here than the North of England. Colder it is however by several degrees.

The coach and its weary occupants eventually arrive in Canet Plage some 26 hours after leaving Preston in Lancashire. The camp site looks very clean and tidy and the welcome from the staff is warm. The temperature however is not and our travel adventure, not just for a few days but as it turns out for the next 20 years, begins.

FIRST DAY IN FRANCE

Now did I mention the Tramontane wind, you know, the one that the brochure didn't? Well, this powerful force of nature certainly was welcoming us with a vengeance. Oh, and that average temperature the brochure promised has turned out to be actually colder than the early morning slight frost we left in Lancashire. I exaggerate a little but it was cold, bitterly cold.

After unpacking our cases in the wooden Swiss chalet type home that we would live in for the duration of our stay we did as we promised and dutifully made our way over to the tour welcome meeting in the camp site bar. As expected, it was mostly stuff we knew already but the one interesting fact about the meeting was that we had just met a key player in the initial part of our stay, it was just that we did not realise it yet.

So, we donned our winter clothes.

Oh, that right we didn't bring any.

Never mind, let's go and explore the area, our home for the next eight days. The Brasilia site looks great, extremely clean and very orderly, but in this temperature there is no one really around so our new surroundings are not coming across as all that inviting just as yet. Wandering just beyond the entrance gates the situation changes dramatically. We find ourselves behind the working dry dock area of Canet Plage marina on what is looking very familiar to us as a basic industrial unit site, very typical of similar sites in the UK – except with boats. The wind is whipping up the most horrendous cloud of dust from the site mixing with sand from the beach and visibility is down to virtually zero. We head around to the beach but the wind is getting stronger and the dense cloud is so low that you can barely make out the sea through the added sandstorm.

Oh, what have we done?

This is just the most awful start to our new French experience. Actually this is just the hors d'oeuvre, the main course turns out to be a real stinker but we are to be spared that for a couple of hours.

I really need to be home and I don't mean my new chalet in France.

Surely that coach we arrived on earlier is still here and has not started to make the return trip back to England and they can simply put us back on it and take us home. The feeling we have of total despair and in being so far from home in what we perceive already as a truly awful place is an overwhelming one. However, on second thoughts this holiday has all been paid for and we Lancastrians always want our monies worth so despite my total reservations about it we decide we will stay and see how this holi-day develops. If I knew at that moment just how we would feel a few hours later then we would be on that coach NOW.

Through the sand and dust and attempting to cover our faces against the ferocious elements we stagger back to the chalet feeling exhausted. It would be good if I was able to say we were exhilar-ated as well but that we are not. We are just cold, windswept and depressed.

It was not meant to be like this, the brochure had promised.

The girl in the travel agent promised.

All the way down on the coach the Holiday Camp girls promised.

The reality that we had found so far was quite different. Did I say we were fed up already? Sorry of course I did.

Also we had no supplies of food; there was not a shop that appeared to be within striking distance. Even Scott of the Antarctic would not have ventured out again for food in that wind. I was certainly not going out for any length of time in that weather again. There was nothing for it but that we head out for the camp site restaurant but it would not be before we had all blocked the shower cubicle with plenty of sand and dust extracted from every crevice imaginable. Freshly scrubbed we could now all head out in what was currently a slightly gentler storm. Things are looking up already.

That's what you think - Ha Ha.

Immediately on arrival in the bar/restaurant we meet the irrepressible Diego and his fiery Spanish wife Sylvie. What a joy Diego will be over the next few days, in fact, over the next few years. The warmth of the welcome makes us all immediately feel better and more at ease. Diego is such a laid back person it is unreal and the contrast with his all action wife, she of the extreme Latin temperament is a sight to behold – and hear. How did they ever meet?

Sylvie is bustling between all the tables and then back to the bar carrying impossible quantities of glasses and all the while continually barking instructions to Diego – get more glasses, more beer, more wine, clean that table, clean the bar, stop talking and on and on. He however only sees his role as host, confidently knowing that he is so impossible attractive both physically and in his personality, he is there to move between tables spreading bonhomie or to do the same hosting at the bar, merrily shaking and swirling cocktails. His pride and joy is his Mont Blanc which he delights in setting fire to at your table, a real eyebrow scorcher. What he absolutely does not see his role being defined as is actually doing anything at speed and certainly not any physical work. However to me this woman is truly knife throwingly dangerous and Deigo is clearly either a very courageous man or incredibly stupid as regards his personal safety.

But she loves him, for the moment.

We enjoyed a drink on the house and then a meal that did not at all disappoint and this helps us to feel more settled and at home and importantly on holiday. One or two more people slowly drift in to the bar. Some of them we recognize from the coach journey and others are tourists from Germany, France and particularly Holland. We soon realize that one of the great joyful activities of being in France is partaking in the people watching. Never having previously been in an environment where there are so many nationalities congregated in one place and all having been thrown together for several days, then this is all new to us and of course the game of people watching will be working both ways. Our Welsh family of new friends from the coach trip along with their several children come in and sit near us and they will be the ones that we bond with during this trip. This situation is now much better and our expectations have grown that this can and will be a wonderful holiday, or at the very least we can forget all about getting straight back on the coach and heading home to England.

Just after finishing the meal my wife Niamh decides that she need to collect something from the chalet and I throw her the key and think nothing more of it. Our chat at the table carries on for all the time she is away and after a couple of glasses of wine I am feeling more relaxed about things starting to be well again with the world.

Suddenly!

Niamh is there looking terrified and almost unable to speak, as white as a sheet.

'What's happened? - What's wrong?'

'There, there is a man in our chalet, he has broken in. I just ran way. Someone help'.

Four of us jumped up scattering chairs as we did so and ran back to the chalet, collecting a member of staff along the way to come with us. Just as we arrived we saw the man running down the beach track away from our open chalet door. Going inside we saw that all had been ransacked and the chalet looked just as if a group of teenagers had been living in it for several weeks.

We have never been burgled before, so anyone who unfortunately has had this traumatic experience will appreciate the feeling of looking at the sorry state of all your possessions having been turned over and trashed in this way. As we sifted through everything the strange thing was that it did not appear that we had lost that much property in his raid. My daughter was missing a couple of items and so was my son but these were replaceable easily and not of any great value, either real of sentimental. The whole thing was strange and surreal. There were some decent items for him to have taken but for whatever reason he had left those behind. So who was this intruder and would he come back? Your thoughts turn to consider a reason as to why he had come. He took very little. Did he specifically want to find one of us? The more you thought the more you realized that we could not sleep here tonight and yes, by now the coach was on its way back to England.

The manager and staff of Brasilia were excellent in their response to the break in and swung into decisive action to help us. They moved all our things out of the trashed chalet and into a brand new large mobile home. Lovely it was too. However this event was all very disconcerting and it was still difficult to see how our holiday could ever recover from this blow. It was certainly impossible to comprehend as to how we would be able to sleep that night. As least we were all safe and nothing much had been lost, so physically and materially little harm was done. We would press on. We would enjoy ourselves. The camp site staff had been so kind, particularly our new friend Diego. You could see that they were all taking this as a very personal affront to their reputation and to their region. They would not let us down and we appreciated that very much. This naturally generous warmth of the Languedoc people we would soon grow to love. Friends would be made this week and at the end of the holiday the desire to return would become overwhelming. That was very much still for the future but they had started to put things right for us, not just materially but more importantly emotionally and that was something to treasure.

Just as we had finished settling into our new surroundings for the night a knock then came to the door of the mobile home. It was very dark by now and it would be true to say that we were certainly still somewhat nervous and twitchy as regards wanting to see anyone else at the door.

When I cautiously answered the door it turned out to be the tour manager who also has been so helpful in this surreal start to our holiday.

She had breaking news.

The perpetrator of this crime had been caught. The local municipal police had caught him sitting on the beach drinking a bottle of our wine and making no attempt at all to hide or to get away from the area.

Incredibly, the burglar was one of the tour representatives that only a few hours earlier had welcomed us so warmly in the bar at that afternoon meeting.

We had been burgled by the people running our holiday.

Really! You could not make it up.

Of all the events that could not be expected to occur then this had to be pretty close to the top of the list. He was English, not French and had been working alongside them during the entire season. We could only assume that something had flipped in his mentality, maybe triggered by being so far away from home. Who knows? What it did mean for us was that we could relax a little now as regards the circumstances of this and that it would appear that we had not in any way been a specific target; he was just after a bit more spending money it seems or even just a comforting bottle of wine.

The tour company were reasonably apologetic but somehow I didn't get the impression they were quite as surprised at this turn of events as we were. I think that at the time we got a free drink out of it or suchlike but they would have to compensate us more when we were back in the UK. That was when I turned into a 'keyboard warrior' and wrote one of my most withering of complaint letters. Actually in the event we got another holiday at little expense and I suppose it may perhaps surprise you that we took up this offer after the start we have had so far but be assured things do begin to look up eventually.

We really didn't sleep much that night but after 24 hours of travelling on the coach and the dreadful events occurring so far in Canet that was of very little surprise. Fortunately M. Argenson and my rouge tete started a complete change in our view of France and that has become a lifelong love of the country and its people. So rest assured there is more to come from these innocents abroad.

OUR FRENCH TRAVEL LOVE AFFAIR BEGINS

Feeling strangely optimistic and adventurous due to sleep deprivation when emerging from my bed on the Saturday morning for our first full day in Languedoc Roussillon I decide we should all go into Perpignan on the local bus. Of course the sensible and safe option would be to go for a gentle walk and explore nearby Canet Plage but as you will have read from the opening of this book an impromptu trip into Perpignan turns out to be a wise choice with lasting consequences for our future enjoyment of French travel.

I say this is adventurous because I have not got a clue as to where the bus leaves from or how you negotiate such a perilous journey on French public transport. From my intensive studies of French language tapes in my car when driving to and from work I do remember the words 'aller retour' denoting to the driver that I will also want to come back from Perpignan later in the day. The helpful Diego informs me as to where the bus departs from and gives me a colour coded timetable map for the bus routes in the area. The bus stop is located across scrubland which is in fact the non-too picturesque walking route into Canet if you decide to continue on over a small bridge straddling a stream that runs out into the harbour. Not terribly attractive purely as a walk but the track gets us there. The one redeeming feature of this stretch of land as a walk is that in the far distance there is an amazing backdrop of the Pyrenees mountain range, still snow-capped in late spring.

Convened at the bus stop are a group of six or seven elderly men and women, stereotypically southern French in character. Shopping bags in hand the market beckons for them and in fact they will only be riding a couple of stops into Canet town rather than shopping in Perpignan. I suspect it is many years since they ventured that far from home. Elderly French residents in this region always have the appearance of having worked on the land all of their life, the men are weather aged in an outdoor working life way and the women give the appearance of having spent their entire lives caring for their menfolk in the kitchen after making this journey to the market every day. They probably mend the cars as well. The men however will not be going shopping. He will meet up with his friends in town and no doubt have a Pastis or a coffee and certainly a smoke in the little town square. I have the feeling that most of the daily domestic work here is reserved exclusively for the women and the men are mere observers, silently wondering how the womenfolk get through all this workload but without stirring any feeling that their conscience could ever persuade them to share that load. It would appear to have been ever thus in this area and I have grown to suspect that the identical division of labour occurs in most of rural France.

These new acquaintances of ours give us a very good silent look over as we stand self-consciously in the bus queue. Actually, as we will learn very quickly the French do not queue, but they do with some rapidity form a fairly effective scrum or ruck at the door of the newly arrived red and yellow bus. We being obedient and programmed as English quietly form an orderly queue of four behind them. I do manage to detect a faint snigger and condescending smile from our little party of elderly shoppers and I suppose on reflection we probably do look a bit like aliens from another planet. I think it may be our newly purchased clothes, freshly worn that very morning that so amuses them. I cannot avoid getting the sense that for them shopping for clothes is not particularly high on their life's agenda. It really isn't for me but sometimes you are persuaded that you must buy something new.

The bus as I say arrives and we stand back or should I say we are brushed aside by these competitive souls. They may be elderly but they are still very active.

After the older ones have squeezed through the narrow door it is finally my turn to have an audience with the driver:

"Quatre aller retour pour Perpinya s'il vous plais".

I had also remembered to use the Catalan form of Perpignan and I do have to say that I am quite proud to have recalled that and it goes down very well indeed with the driver who is so impressed that he lifts his head from its disinterested position resting on his hand. I can also hear a gentle murmur of approval and sense a nodding of heads from our fellow travellers. They would probably let me buy a house here now. I am at one with them.

It is hard to over emphasise the pride the people of this region have in being resolutely Catalan even though they are geographically still firmly in France. They have no conception of being French citizens first and would be most offended if you implied that they were. The people here are Catalans through and through and this is a strange quirk of the region, almost an unofficial declaration of independence that goes somewhat unchallenged. Road signs particularly here are also in Catalan as are most other information signs and if they are not then someone will soon turn them into Catalonian with a tin of paint and a brush. The Catalan language is spoken quite widely here and their French dialect is spoken with such a strong regional accent that it can be really hard to follow but by contrast we have found that many are prepared to speak English if required. Funnily enough, we have found over the years that the further you are from the English Channel the more people seem to speak English or should I say are prepared to speak it. The most resistance to helping you out with the language seems to us to have been in Normandy for some reason, the closest area to England. Having read several books about D-Day and the price the inhabitants paid for the liberation of Normandy I perhaps can be more understanding about that reticence.

Anyway bus tickets in hand and a feeling that my 'passport' had been mentally stamped we head for a group of seats filtering by the now beaming smiles of approval from the other passengers. I think now I just need to don a Perpignan rugby shirt or if not then perhaps a Barcelona soccer shirt and then I will probably get a free drink in town.

Travelling by bus in France and in this area in particular is quite a different experience than when using public transport in England. Perhaps the best way for me to describe it is that it feels as if you are travelling on a road network that has been designed like a children's roadway play mat. The bus will constantly pull off the main road onto what seem to be parallel roads to the main highway and these have random drop off points for passengers before going under or over the highway and back on another parallel road before re-joining the direct route. The many roundabouts too have this quirk where you do not go the way you expect to go but the bus heads off by an extra exit to run once again along a parallel road that to be honest seems quite unnecessary. What this does do though is make it feel as if you are really travelling on a dedicated route, just as on the child's play mat and you never have an interruption, no possibility of encountering any traffic hold up, a sense of travel similar to feeling like you are really on a tram. This layout would not be possible in England but here they have the space to design roads in a more efficient but decidedly quirky way.

The most recognizable landmark that comes into view as we travel into the centre of Perpignan is Le Castillet, a 14th-century gateway tower that also now contains the Casa Pairal museum of local history and Catalan culture. This I decide is where we should get off and start to explore Perpignan.

The weather today is just as the brochure so clearly promised - extremely hot. It seems that just as surely as I had not packed any winter clothes I had not packed a sun hat. I don't know if you are the same, ever so slightly follically thin on top but if you are you will understand, that I always seem to think that if I make sure to walk on the shady side of the street I will be OK. The problem is that the majority of the shops Niamh wants to see are on the sunny side and also in France there will always be a square at the end of the street and this will have very little shade so any attempt to get by without a hat I have to be frank is plain stupid. Anyway for now I stick with my theory and get gently roasted by the piercing sun.

One of the indisputable things about French towns is that they have infinitely more independent shops in them than in England. Almost every high street in England has pretty much the same formula of chain shops, cafés and restaurants. Some have very few if any cafés and restaurants for lunch. Yes my home town of Blackburn I am talking about you. Yes, before you write in I know there are some fine examples of towns that have fought very hard to keep their independent shops and they are not only to be commended but supported. I love for instance driving around Suffolk and Norfolk and being able to count on one hand the number of supermarkets whereas in Lancashire for instance I need a calculator to count them. It is all very sad, and I am speaking with some authority as the excellent independent store, part of the business I worked in for over four decades, was forced into closure by the lack of foresight of town planners greedy for instant rate returns. Don't get me started.

Niamh loves the choice of shops and the variety of products in Perpignan. To be honest I do to. Having battled greedy commerce for many years in England it always makes me so happy to see the way the French have to a large extent protected their towns and villages. Speaking of chain shops however one shop you will always find in any sizable town in France is L'Occitane selling perfume and other assorted fragrant goodies. This is Niamh's absolute favourite and most irresistible of stores. Despite howls of protest from my wallet we always have to go inside a L'Occitane. The inevitable problem is that in contrast to say L'Occitane in Covent Garden or the Trafford Centre Manchester where the service is absolutely fine, don't get me wrong, is that when you go into a French store the charm is cranked up substantially so that as the sales assistant is talking your credit cards start virtually to be leaping out of your wallet so eager are you to buy. The extra sales pitch for me is that they also have a men's range so the charm starts on me too so we always end up purchasing double.

The delights of the L'Occitane store are only the beginning however but for now I am exhausted already – and hot.

This now takes us back to the beginning of our story and the café-bar Le Malassis and the wonderful M. Argenson. Following the relief he applied to my head we had coffees and coca colas for the teenagers and took in the ambiance of not just this charming café but the narrow street itself and the vibrant life on it, in our view contrasting greatly with our rather greyer subdued streets back home. We are not to be sitting there very long as apparently there is much more shopping still to do. On leaving, we read the menu placed outside the café door and simply because of the warmth of our welcome and the ambiance we decide that we must return for lunch. On we go to the shops.

Shopping in Perpignan is clearly cheering everyone up after the most awful start to our trip. I though am eager for a bit of culture and so I leave the girls to their wandering of the streets and browsing the shops.

From Rue Louis Blanc I work my way down Rue Saint Jean leading into Place Leon Gambetta. It is from here that you get your first view of Perpignan Cathedral or to give the building its full title, Basilique-Cathedral de Saint Jean Baptiste. From the entrance to this square the Cathedral does not look all that imposing; in fact it gives the appearance despite its size of having been squeezed into the end of the square as an afterthought. The approach that you walk down of Place Gambetta is also not really giving off the impression that you are confronting a building that is in fact architecturally very interesting and well worth a visit. Down the approach to the Cathedral you pass a hairdresser, a florist, a couple of nondescript shops and numerous apartment entrances with their rows of doorbells and letter boxes. The final establishment on the right hand side just before the Cathedral entrance and almost impossible to exclude when you take a photograph is a funeral directors - 'Pompes Funerbres'. Of course, being my cynical self I can only assume that they are on good terms with the priests or vice versa. Not really the most reassuring outlet you want to see before entering the Cathedral but again quite typically French, always mixing styles and uses for buildings in the form of a melting pot. Inside the Cathedral however there is much to catch the eye as you wander around this medieval structure that was built from 1324 and converted to its present form in the 15th century. Perpignan Cathedral is very typically

Catalan in style as is so much of the architecture of the town of Perpignan. I assume the surrounding clutter of the more modern buildings were constructed much later and it is a pity that the Cathedral does not still stand alone, proudly away from all the additional unnecessary distraction of these surrounding buildings. Immediately next door to the left of the Cathedral entrance is the restaurant Le Saint Jean (original choice of name). This lovely restaurant has many tables set out in the shaded courtyard abutting right up the Cathedral wall. We did some years later eat here at a table placed right against the Cathedral wall. I try to visualize a scene where that could be the case next to Westminster Abbey. Here it does not seem in any way incongruous to the French. We savoured a wonderful meal here on a lovely balmy evening but the location somehow seemed wrong in that it intruded on the space that surely was the Cathedrals alone in times past. I get the same sense of bad planning when you try to locate St Pauls Cathedral on the London skyline from the river, much is now virtually obscured. Certainly you have to feel that less is more in architecture but the land grab of commerce will always win out and certainly in this part of Perpignan it is true.

I start to retrace my steps back to our starting point arriving once again at Le Castillet, where we alighted from the bus, wandering briefly around this 14th Century gatehouse tower. Although it also now houses a small museum you get the best out of visiting it by simply viewing the outside structure and it is one of essential photo opportunities in Perpignan. Viewing Le Castillet also leads your eye over the Pont Magenta and takes your gaze down the twin quays Vauban and Carnot. This is Perpignan at its most attractive best, especially on a hot sunny day like today. There are a host of cafés and coffee bars amongst the shops situated along the quays, all giving a happy southern vibe to the lively and colourful Perpignan. Separating the quays is the gentle Bassa River that gives the appearance of a canal, a very pleasant place to observe on a stroll down the quays or to sit beside for a while. On the side of the quays are grassy banks sloping gently down to the river interspersed with colourful flowers beds. The feature colours of the flowers are typically the colours of the Catalan flag as are most things here. It seems that they do actually allow the French flag to be flown occasionally but here we are most definitely in Catalonia.

There will be time again to explore Perpignan and do it justice but it is now time for me to catch up with the shoppers. I easily find Niamh and Charlotte by the Bijouterie Ducommun admiring as usual some fabulous jewellery, in particular the necklaces that use the garnets that Perpignan is famous for. More on that later. At that precise moment we are startled by a clock bell striking 12 noon and then the window and door shutters of the shop this clanging clock is attached to make an even more jarring sound by dropping down with great velocity and noise. Our lesson number one about travelling in France - everything stops for lunch and even though many potential customers may be thronging the streets and looking in your shop window displays it is most certainly time for a leisurely two hour lunch. This is mandatory and lunch is taken very seriously. I was just very thankful that my head was not peering into the shop boasting the shutters as these had every appearance of being a capable guillotine substitute. So for us and everyone else lunch it is, we happily go with the flow and act as the locals do. Everything stops.

As we stroll back to Le Malassis I have opportunity to digress once again into my love of architecture but in this instance architecture that is presented in the most bizarre fashion and an example that would make our architecture obsessed British Prince Charles apoplectic with rage. I can only begin to imagine the forceful opinions he would express if he came upon La Loge de Mere higher up this pedestrianized street.

La Loge de Mere is set within a beautiful square and this building also dates in construction from a similar time period to the Cathedral and architecturally you can clearly see the typical Catalan influence. It is a stunning building that although clearly Catalan would not be out of place in an Italian Renaissance square. It looks especially good when viewed from within the square with the adjacent statues also helping the composition of the area. Where it does not look so pleasing is the view at eye level from Rue Louis Blanc. Incredibly it has been turned into a fast food restaurant and the claim on the signage that it is 'particularly good for children' gives you the picture. It surely could only happen in France. The French have this strange mixture of design thought whereby they are dedicatedly preserving buildings and monuments for posterity in a wonderful way then also by total contrast they are also prepared to allow some of these gorgeous buildings to be used in the most inappropriate way imaginable. Over the years that we have returned to visit Perpignan we have sort of got used to La Loge but that does not alter the fact that this is a crime against the building.

A letter to 'The Times' Prince Charles.

We move on averting our eyes down to Rue Alsace Lorraine and approach the entrance to Le Malassis.

AND SO TO OUR FIRST LUNCH IN FRANCE – FIRST OF VERY MANY

F rom the open doorway we tentatively peer inside the restaurant and see the busy M.Argenson cooking inside a very hot steamy kitchen with his African sous chef working alongside him. M.Argenson's rather formidable wife is waiting behind the typical well stocked old wooden zinc topped bar just to the right of the entrance. A young, friendly and can I say on behalf of my son a stunningly attractive young waitress immediately comes up to greet us. This is a fine start and Le Malassis is just the sort of place I had hoped to find on our first exploration into the art of French dining.

We are seated at the allocated table and yes, it

does have the expected checked table cloths and yes, the waitress does immediately bring a carafe of water. It is all so stereotypically French – it is delightful. I take off my cap, oh, sorry no I still haven't got one. I actually begin to mop my brow to the amusement of M. Argenson who is looking over his shoulder at our party from the kitchen. He comes out after having handed his hot pan over to his assistant and warmly shakes my hand and reserves his kisses for the ladies. Although the waitress is attentive and capable he is happy to explain the menu himself and then hand us over to the young lady, not before insisting we have a carafe of Rosé wine for the table.

We have already decided on what we wish to order for lunch and the charming mademoiselle brushes a slender hand across her hair as she first of all asks our son what is his heart's desire. Unfortunately and entirely due to her extreme attractiveness he is unable to speak. This condition applies to English as well as French so I quickly step in and decide to order for him. He has already resolved that he would happily stay here and follow her life's journey but sadly this must be a brief encounter. How many times does that happen in France?

For myself, I order conservatively and safely for

my very first French meal – omelettes fines herbes with a bowl of frites. Good choice.

Niamh orders a goat's cheese salad. I am really not a fan of goat's cheese. For me it is too goaty. Oh, come on you know what I mean.

Niamh loves this pungent cheese and especially the intense French versions of this particular variety which varies in flavour and strength from region to region but you will find that goat's cheese in France is just as popular as Cheddar cheese in England.

Charlotte plays safe also and orders a croque monsieur, which is basically a ham and cheese toastie although the French tend to try to elevate it to a higher gastronomic level.

I see my omelette being rolled for plating and when it arrives it is just perfect. One of the benchmarks that many famous chefs use when deciding to hire a new chef in their kitchens is to test how well they can cook an omelette. Get it right and they get the job. Cooking the perfect omelette is not as easy as we amateurs cooks tend to think and no doubt like myself you have had or made some firm rubbery ones in your time.

There are no mistakes here, this omelette is superbly cooked, just on the point of being set and a little gentle in colour on the outside, still soft and oozing at the centre , flavoured with an excellent balance of herbs. The fresh green herbs are as is usual in this French omelette - parsley, chives, tarragon and chervil. Delicious.

The omelette is accompanied with a bowl of the very best French fries I have ever tasted. No, I must insist that they must be the best anyone will ever have tasted. Charlotte certainly thinks so as she keeps taking a handful from my bowl as her meal has not come with any such accompaniment.

All the while M.Argenson has been observing the scene and watching her stealing my fries, then he busies himself once again in his kitchen. Within a few minutes he comes out from the open kitchen to our table carrying a large bowl of fresh fries and places them down in front of Charlotte. Her eyes light up in delight and so does his at seeing her obvious pleasure and her thanks for getting such a treat. Le Malassis is a generous place that is full of warmth and pleasure. As I have described this meal you can appreciate that it is in fact only a simple lunch but this restaurant firmly sets a standard for us to use on our future travels and thankfully in the intervening years we have found many such places throughout France. These café/bar/restaurants will be fairly humble and generally run by one chef that will deliver the most pleasingly simple food reflecting that particular region and punch well above their weight in giving pleasure to the diner.

In between all this frites activity Niamh's goat's cheese salad had been brought out by M.Argenson and I have to say it was hard to ignore the very huge smile on his face as he presented this dish in front of her. As he set the plate down I recoiled in my chair as if someone had just sprayed some ammonia or incredibly strong bleach on the table. The strength and goaty power of this cheese was breath taking in a very literal sense.

His smile said it all, 'You like goats cheese, well let's see how you get on with this one, Ha Ha.' (In French)

He turned and headed back to his open kitchen, his large shoulders rising and falling with laughter. He and his able assistant were giggling like two young schoolchildren who had just placed a whoopee cushion on the teachers chair.

I said at a moment when I could breath, "There is no way in this world that you can eat that. I don't think I can even stay sat next to you with that on the table. It needs to go outside"

Niamh said "I can and I will, just watch".

Do you know what? She ate every single morsel of it.

How she did that I will never know as I can say categorically I could not even have tried a small bite of it.

The kitchen audience looked on as Niamh unhesitatingly ate the dish, a smile of pleasure and satisfaction on her face, a face that was turned in the direction of the kitchen. Absolutely no sign of the immense pain I was sure she must be in. She genuinely wasn't at all discomforted. She enjoyed her meal and looking back she has eaten many similar strength goat cheeses over the years and I have had to sit there observing and taking in the aroma.

This incredible culinary feat of Niamh showed M. Argenson and his staff that it was our intention when here in France to engage with their food and culture and along with our attempts at speaking French it sealed a lasting friendship as we continued to return over many years to this café bar, always welcomed and recognised even though it could be a couple of years in between visits. By contrast, you can visit a supermarket café in England every single day of the year and order the same thing and probably be asked by the same person on every subsequent time as to what you want without being offered a flicker of recognition. That makes the level of service at a humble place such as this so lovely and rewarding, something you will happily travel a long way to keep experiencing.

After finishing our carafe or two of local Rosé wine and our ice cream deserts we bid a warm farewell but assure them all that we will return later in the week and of course we do, repeating almost exactly the very same meal we have enjoyed on this our very first meal in a French restaurant.

◆ ◆ ◆

The time is getting very close to 2 o'clock by now but the shops are still closed except for a rebellious cheap clothing store just along the street and also the pharmacy next door to the café. Presumably people need indigestion tablets at lunch so some exceptions can be made. As we turn back into Rue Louis Blanc we hear the unmistakeable sound of the clock and then the shop front shutters crashing back upwards signalling that all shopping can now restart. Everyone has been fed and watered, people are a little sleepy perhaps but they will try to serve you with your intended purchases now. To us it is very odd how all of this routine works. For a full two hours the whole activity in the centre of Perpignan comes to a stop except for the pavement cafés. Then precisely on 2 o'clock it is as if time restarts and the whole place is once again alive and vibrant with shoppers and the pleasant hum of people finishing their long lunch. This is not the English way but then again this is the beauty of travel and even at this early stage in our travels it is clear that you will always get the best out of your trip by embracing the local culture wholeheartedly. A carafe of chilled wine at 12 o'clock is certainly a fine incentive for me to stop shopping, not that I need much incentive. Another carafe at 2 o'clock would encourage me not to restart.

We start to explore down the side streets that lead away from the centre of the town and come upon the Serge Blanco clothing store which was launched by the famous French Rugby Union full back, a sport I love to watch and I have greatly admired his style of play over the years. The great man is actually stood outside the store but I still don't trust my French language skills sufficiently to approach him. His brand at the time is in its infancy on this visit to Perpignan but it goes on to be an expensive global brand. Should have got the shirt.

While I am distracted and star struck Niamh and Charlotte manage to find yet another jewellers shop. Actually, that is not too difficult here in Perpignan. If there is one speciality store that Perpignan is not short of then you would have to say that it was jewellers and there are many fine ones here. This one that the girls have now found specializes in Lalique, that very high quality French glassware that began to be produced by Rene Lalique in Paris in the late 19th century. This particular jeweller sells a range of necklaces and earrings created by Lalique and it is understating it to say that the girls find these baubles very attractive. Once more the service in the store is very attentive but without making you feel overly pressurised and it is not long before a purchase is made. The opaque blue glass necklace and earrings are unarguably beautiful and by the standards of today's Lalique prices these turn out to be a sensible purchase. These gems are still as beautiful today over 20 years later.

It is now time for us to return to Canet Plage and to Brasilia but on this short visit I have already grown to love Perpignan, warts and all. It has a generous Catalan warmth to it; certainly a rough-ness around the edges particularly if you stray out of the centre but even in these places there is plenty of architecture to admire lining the old winding streets. Off the beaten track Perpignan has a slight air of danger to be sure but we have never once found it in reality to be so. The people are warm and friendly, a striking mix of the wealthy fashionable 'beautiful' people alongside the more humble Cata-lans who as families have no doubt resided here for generations and are so eager to please a visitor in the shops and cafés and the open markets that are dot-ted around the town. We will return later this week but will also develop a passion for the place and region meaning that we will come back independ-ently by TGV some years later and explore the area more fully. I will write of that later but do come and visit.

Once we are back at Brasilia we are informed that the tour representatives have arranged a flying visit to a local supermarket so that we can all stock up our supplies and in a small way have another opportunity to immerse ourselves in French life particularly for those that have not yet been outside the camp site – some never do. It is a good idea and most of us decide to take up the offer.

The supermarket Intermarche is not that far from the camp site and the local shoppers seem a bit bemused that we have the opinion that their shop is worth a coach trip. You will discover that French supermarkets are not like the generic ones you are used to at home. The range of goods on offer is nowhere near as extensive (which is absolutely fine by me) and the major difference is that they also make a real effort to offer as much local produce as they possibly can. That most certainly means the absolute minimum of English products. So if you want Baked Beans, Tomato sauce, Marmite, OXO cubes or any other of your essential British staples you will be sorely disappointed. French supermarkets also have a unique aroma to them, not unpleasant at all but different to ones back home. The closest I can get to an equivalent is to say that if you have experienced going into one of the new Lidl Supermarkets in Western Europe, the ones that have their own bakery just inside the entrance. That smell on entering is as similar as I can describe it.

These supermarkets offer a wide variety of local vegetables and fruits - in this region of Roussillon that especially means freshly picked apricots and cherries. These wonderful fragrant fruits along with the succulent melons are to be found everywhere in this region and are often sold at simple roadside stalls by the producers themselves. There is one offering of produce that is so glaringly different from anything seen in supermarkets at home and that is the fish counter. Or should I say the fish aisle. This vast stainless steel counter stretches down the full depth of the store. Any conceivable fish or seafood that you can imagine is here on display and offered to you at reasonable prices. Back home in England I very often hear people say that they do not cook with or eat fish because they cannot abide the smell. I always tell them that fresh fish does not have an unpleasant smell and the main thing that you notice here in the French supermarket is that there is absolutely no smell, fishy or otherwise. You could happily have tables set out alongside the fish counter and you could eat your evening meal by this display at no detriment to your enjoyment of the meal. It really is that fresh and clean. We readily select some cod, bream and king prawns and look forward to cooking them for our lunch tomorrow.

We also find that the meat section of the supermarket differs greatly from home and it is here that you need to exercise a little care in making your selection. The butchery skills displayed in French supermarkets are not as precise as you will find in England, definitely a bit rough and ready compared to back home. This can make a lot of the prepared meat look slightly unappealing but the actual quality is very good. They also seem to have lamb chops from sheep that have much larger rib cages than ours in England. Probably the sheep are prepared at an older age than lamb back home, tending to be more closely related to mutton than young lamb. Still, they are full of flavour and tender when cooked.

There is one French word that you do really need to have learnt before you go food shopping in a supermarket or on a French street market. That word is - Cheval. Certainly, the meat labelled 'cheval' looks absolutely succulent and tempting and the colour not displeasing. However, unless you eaten this before and are happy to taste it again then horse I would assume is not really your favoured meat of choice. Years later I very nearly accidentally bought some on a Provencal market and had to scurry away in total embarrassment as realisation dawned at the point of when it had come to be my turn at the front of the queue. Not for me thank you.

French supermarkets do have their fair share of bland and pretty quirky over prepared products that are best avoided but the one product range that they do win hands down with as opposed to English offerings is in the wine section. Wherever you go in France you will always find a wonderful range of wines, these will be predominantly local but offered at amazing prices. If you love your Rosé wine then this Southern region of France is the place to be. Most of the wines on display here are from the South of France including Provence with a small section devoted to other French regions. And a really tiny apologetic section dedicated to non-French wines. Of the resurgent English wines there is not a trace. This plentiful feast for the eyes and palate is a fine addition to our fledgling wine education and we are happy and eager pupils indeed.

All stocked up we head back to spruce up our appearance for the evening.

THE REMARKABLE JACQUES - OUR EVENINGS ENTERTAINMENT

We are back at the camp site after successfully negotiating our first foray into French public transport and supermarkets and having had a thoroughly enjoyable day that has begun to restore our confidence in the merits of this trip. We see on passing by that tonight in the bar restaurant there is to be entertainment. Now for me the thought of communal entertainment provided by failed would be stars of stage and screen fills me with total dread. A visit to the dentist would seem to be almost as preferable. Oh and there is bound to be karaoke. Yes, I am unapologetically a snob as regards the music and entertainment that I enjoy. Let's just say I really don't go for easy listening and tribute acts and I definitely don't go for people showing how badly they can sing at other people expense. In this view I am of course outnumbered three to one as regards having a quiet evening in but I console myself that I can hide in a corner with another carafe of wine. So we all put on another set of fresh new clothes and head out into the night. The teenagers have already made new friends and they hurry off before us to get the evening started.

We pass Mathieu on our way to the bar. Young Mathieu I can only assume is related to the owners as his actual working role appears to have no purpose but he is always seemingly very busy riding around the camp site on his bicycle. He is cheery in his greeting as always but just what he actually does is a complete mystery. He comes across in appearance to be a little geeky, perhaps one for the video games but appearances can be very deceptive as we will find out later.

We arrive at the bar to be greeted by Diego with his cocktail menu which I am becoming skilled at resisting. I look over to the stage at the far end and raise my eyebrows in pondering the delights to come. How totally wrong I would turn out to be in my generalization of what can be provided in the name of entertainment in these places. Brasilia turns out to be very much a cut above.

As Diego passes me my usual – a carafe of local Rosé - some familiar strains of music make me turn back towards the stage. The familiar opening bars of the Eagles 'Take it Easy' are being played. It was a very welcome comforting sound and so in tune with making us feel happier in our surroundings and more than that it was being sung and played incredibly well and professionally.

Jacques we would come to know extremely well over the years but tonight was the first occasion we had sampled his residency at Brasilia and we would come to love his music that he played and sang for the adults but also the supporting way he had with the children and teenagers with his 'Crazy Dancing' slots. We settle around a table populated with a few familiar faces and the teenagers are very happily getting along with others of varying nationalities in an exceptionally happy environment. The next carafe tonight is Sangria of course and that is brought over by Sylvie, Diego's wife. I am sure she is carrying about 6 carafes and at the same time writing down orders and taking payment, giving the money change from her waist belt. She also finds time to scream at Diego to do some work. Diego of course feels he is fully fulfilling the role he was put on the earth to do and totally ignores her. She gets somewhat more physical with her orders to him when she arrives back behind the bar. As I said before he is a brave man but has such a totally different disposition than Sylvie, a woman who is all Latin fiery temperament as exemplified by her jet black hair and olive-skinned complexion. He is just a basically fun guy, so very laid back that he does not even appear to notice Sylvie stomping around and barking orders to him. You really do have to wonder how they met and certainly as to how they ever came to an arrangement to get married. There is one thing that they most certainly do have in common and that is the most beautiful daughter, the two year old Sophie. Diego dotes on her and Sylvie breaks away from time to time to give her attention. You would never put Diego and Sylvie together but you have to admit you are glad they did become a couple when you see Sophie playing and being softly sweet with the people around her. We see Sylvie in the afternoons carrying her back to the house that they have on the camp site, an afternoon sleep so that she is ready to cast her charm in the evening.

Jacques play a few songs to set the mood, he

is particularly accomplished with his Beatles repertoire, before he makes the stage set ready for his
'Crazy Dancing' session, this is the part of the evening that the youngsters have all been looking forward to.

What he is able to achieve better than anyone I
have ever come across is to make this part of the
evening so inclusive for whatever ages the young
ones are at. It is quite a talent to be able to do this,
so often when you are at a wedding or function
and you will all have been there won't you, have
the young ones ended in tears or the older ones
lost interest in the entertainment and the whole
thing falls totally flat. Jacques somehow has this
special skill and personality to hold all their attention throughout and the joy and pleasure radiating
off these children makes such a warm atmosphere
throughout the hall. The parents carry on contentedly having a beer or a glass of wine and so enjoying
seeing their young ones having such a great time.

Jacques makes this all work by selecting ones
from all age groups to be helpers in the entertainment during the week and it is this inclusivity that
builds a young team spirit that works fabulously.
This is deceptively a lot of work though because he

will have to do this again and again throughout the season as new people arrives. I read an online review of Brasilia some 10 years later just after Jacques had just left for pastures new and the people who wrote it were so sad that he was no longer there and saying that the entertainment although decent was just standard fare and not the special blend that Jacques offered. He is still plying his special brand of entertainment in the Roussillon area and maybe we can see him again in the future with our Granddaughter Ronelle – she would just love it.

For the teenagers he will end this part of the evening with some sort of show that they present, perhaps a boy or girl band made up of the holiday-makers or a musical sketch. Once again he is able to mix all the different nationalities to work together. Our son James was in one of his boy bands – I headed for the toilets out of earshot. Actually he seemed to be doing OK when I had the courage to come back out and watch.

If there is just one thing that I have to hold against Jacques it is the way he gives in to the constant requests to play that ubiquitous holiday tune of the 90's - La Macarena, and then encouraging the dancing that accompanies it. Back home in England there was a toy cuddly monkey on the market that sang and danced to the Macarena. Charlotte bought one. Twenty years later I can have my head on the pillow trying to sleep and that tune can still even now start swirling around my brain. Thanks Jacques.

When the young ones are satisfied and quite tired Jacques seamlessly moves on to his entertainment spot aimed at the parents and older ones. His repertoire is very wide and eclectic and he can effortlessly sing and speak in several languages. The atmosphere as he progresses the evening along is very mellow.

Diego is getting even mellower much to the disgust of his hardworking wife. His speciality and pleasure is definitely his cocktails and he relentlessly works the tables to try to wear down your resistance. Most eventually do give in to his sales pitch. He particularly wants you to order his Mont Blanc cocktail as that gives him the opportunity to set fire to your table. It is difficult to resist letting him have this moment as it makes him so happy, it makes his wife fume if you will pardon the pun.

Later in the week we enjoy another wonderful evening and stay around until it is quite late but

Jacques is happy to carry on with the music and there is a very chilled atmosphere around the bar. The time has got towards midnight and Jacques has finally stopped playing but after a drink at the bar he comes to ask if we want to go down to the beach bar. For us this is late, well past our bedtime but it is a gorgeous balmy evening so we look at each other and it is definitely a case of - why not? He rounds up a few others of varying nationalities and takes us all outside where he has a pickup truck waiting as our transport. If you had told me a few days earlier that I and my family would be getting into a strange vehicle sans seat belts, going who knows where, with someone I hardly know I would have been a bit disbelieving to say the least. But France, Jacques and Brasilia have worked their charm and we will never regret immersing ourselves in the spirit of the time and place both now and in times to come in a country we are rapidly growing to love.

The pickup makes a journey over some very bumpy terrain, through the sand dunes and yes, in the distance there really is a beach bar. Diego is already there, Sylvie his wife is not, I assume she is looking after the young one although I feel it is just as likely that she thinks this is all too frivolous.

This early part of the morning is just magical under a clear sky with the stars dotting the sky so brightly and extensively visible, in sharp contrast to our occasional view of them in the night sky back home. Another glass of wine is offered and we sit on the beach just able to make out in the moonlight the waves gently lapping onto the shore with the Canet harbour lights just twinkling beyond the outer harbour wall. James and Charlotte are so enjoying this, able to mingle with some young ones of different nationalities in a completely safe environment. I can't help thinking that it is sad to contrast the behaviour we unfortunately see regularly in Britain when a night out with drinking involved seems to have to end in tears when so many over indulge. Here all is enjoyed within unspoken boundaries that enable young and old to enjoy a long evening together in a very convivial way. It is a very special memory that I can still visualize and almost taste the atmosphere of that night, yes very special and it feels worth making the trip for this alone. It is clear though that the lift by pickup transport back to the bar will not be for some time and at around 2 am we decide that it is time to bring to a close to a truly lovely day and find the comfort of our beds. As we are walking back through the warm sand dunes it is a quite beautiful surreal experience and we have a very deep sleep with sweet dreams indeed.

FURTHER FRENCH EDUCATION

O ver the last couple  of years prior to starting our travels to France we had begun to nurture an interest in wine and this would grow to something of an obsession over the next few years but I can assure you it was a very enjoyable passion. I can remember the days and come on admit it so can you, when you ordered a bottle of Mateus Rosé in a restaurant thinking you were so much more of a wine connoisseur than those sad people at the next table who had Blue Nun on their table. I can also remember a bottle of white called Crown of Crowns Liebfraumilch. If your budget could run to ordering that bottle then you were really showing that you knew your stuff when it came to the fruits of the vine. Come to think of it they are the only three wines I can actually remember being aware of back then in the 70's. You never drank wine at home however, only when you went out to a restaurant and that wasn't very often. For us over the last couple of years that ignorance had all started to change.

For some reason, I say that because cooking is not really a sport and that was all I was interested in viewing, I found myself watching the British chef Rick Stein on his very first TV series about fish cookery and allied to that was cooking by Keith Floyd a chef mate of his and both were not averse to extolling the virtues of French wine and demonstrating how to empty a glass. I liked the way they made it appear that cooking could only be achieved to the required standard with a glass of wine in your hand. I got curious due to his enthusiasm and simplicity of cooking and along with getting a passion for fish cookery I soon found that I too always cooked better with a glass of wine near at hand. It was by now much easier in England to obtain a good variety of French wine and we started to enjoy white wines from the Loire Valley in particular. That passion we gained for the wines of that region and also from Burgundy we would develop more fully in a few years' time on some organized wine tours and then by travelling independently with my 16 wine case capacity car. I will write of that another time as it is really a separate subject and one that has given us a vast amount of pleasure. I hope you stay with me for another book as it is a fine journey to recreate.

On the camp site there is a general shop that sells most things you could possibly need including wine, a boulangerie, a butchers shop that does some freshly made ready meals as well as meat and a hairdressers and a couple of other little shop units. There is also a little well stocked wine shop. It is in this wine cave that our real journey into the joys, complexities and variety of French wine begins. This little shop with its passionate owner is a treasure trove of new discoveries, mostly from the Languedoc Roussillon area. They also dispense wine via the petrol pump method at incredibly low prices, less than an English pound a bottle but you have to buy 5 litres and that takes a bit of drinking before it goes a bit flat in flavour – I need more friends. The bottles although not as cheap as at the pump are still exceptional value compared to prices back in the UK. There are no UK taxes here. What this price structure and choice does achieve is give you the chance to try several different types from around this beautiful region and as they say in wine circles you do get to experience the terroir of the Languedoc. The guy in the shop is rightly proud of his little wine boutique and happy to speak at length about the wines of the region and with the hope that he can impart the same passion to you and that you will enjoy the choices he is guiding you towards. We visit him every day and he succeeds completely in his desire to pass on his love of these wines and for us it is this growing knowledge that will develop our interest and love of French wines for many years to come. Thank you little shop for that.

Diego sadly, did not despite his enthusiasm leave us with a great love of French cocktails but for us to take away from here such a discovery of what different varieties of wine there were out there compared to the choice back home was a great joy. It also was apparent that the French keep the best of the vintages for consumption in France, a fact that would become ever apparent in the years to come. I can prove this by one simple question : Our favourite wine is white Sancerre – Has anyone tasted a better one in the UK than they did in and around Sancerre? I rest my case.

◆ ◆ ◆

The little wine shop was not the only place that we had a further education in French wine. Just on the edge of Canet Plage there was a wine producer that we were able to pay a visit to. Chateau L'Esparrou is a beautiful typical French Chateau that has been producing superb wines for 200 years and for us to be visiting such a place for the very first time was to a degree daunting as we felt so lacking in wine knowledge and substantially out of our depth. This first visit was an organized trip by the tour company so having someone else with us to do the talking and coordinating the tastings was very helpful. Chateau L'Esparrou produces a range of AOP Cotes Du Roussillon and also wines made outside of the French 'appellation controle' system allowing them the freedom to produce wines exactly how they would like and so we are back as often we are in France to that mysterious word 'terroir'. The winemaker at this chateau exploits that mineral quality of this sun baked land so very well. Lovely sweet wines - Vins doux naturels, also are here to be tasted. As I said before it is quite daunting to be for the first time in such a grand place tasting wine but the people are so friendly and hospitable that you are soon put at ease and in years to come we would call in unannounced at such places throughout France and have the most wonderful experiences. This is our first encounter with wine tasting but it will not be our last. Of course as new inexperienced tourists we fall for the wine themed souvenirs on offer rather than just concentrating on the wines. We buy a fair selection of the range of wines we have tasted which we will be able to secrete into our luggage to get them back home to England but we also cannot resist buying a formed glass bottle full of wine that is painted quite gaudily and in the shape of a lower arm and hand. What were we thinking of I am not sure but it is still around somewhere all these years later. I like to think our tastes have developed but there was no harm in having a bit of fun.

We so enjoyed the visit that we walk all the way out to the Chateau again a couple of days later and the lady recognises us and is very happy to give us another tasting and we buy a couple more bottles.

When we get back to our camp site home after the walk in the hot southern sun we are certainly glad of a chilled glass of Chateau L'Esparrou Rosé.

It is not my intention when setting out to write this memoir for this book to be a specific tour guide but if I can inspire you to visit one or two places, whether a restaurant we have enjoyed or a wine producer I will name names. Sadly, of course after some 20 years some are now closed and also I cannot guarantee that the standards are the same but we all take that chance when taking on new experiences. Certainly we have found that deciding on your own choices is so much fun and when you discover an absolute gem of a restaurant or winery then you will remember that moment forever. You can make poor choices in France it is true but we have found that trusting your instincts and taking a little care generally rewards you extremely well. The often repeated advice of observing where the locals eat and drink is perfectly true. That certainly is a lesson well learned on this first trip to France.

COLLIOURE – JEWEL OF THE SOUTH

We first set eyes on the beauty that is Collioure on an evening trip along the coast to the town in the tour company's mini bus. This was a slightly unnerving trip of some 20 miles with a somewhat unconvincing driver on a bus packed full of fellow travellers. If the journey out to Collioure was unnerving it was nothing compared with the trip back to Brasilia. That is a few hours hence but before we take that fraught journey home we discover a place that is still in our hearts as perhaps our favourite location anywhere. Yes, it is that beautiful and the people so warm that to sit on a restaurant terrace by the harbour, with that stunning view is quite incomparable. Total bliss.

The full beauty of Collioure will be revealed later in the week and in years to come, on this mild clear evening the sun is going down, the scene is enlightened by the lights of the harbour front cafés and bars and the spot lights focused on Collioure's church, Notre-Dame-des-Anges, a former converted lighthouse. There is of course in this gorgeous setting the natural moonlight sparkling on the sea and reflected on the brightly coloured fishing boats that are such a feature of the harbour at Collioure. These small boats have inspired so many artists over the years being painted and photographed so often that they are synonymous with this beautiful harbour and in the full light of day we will see them at their best later in the week. Artists and artisans such as Andre Derain, Henri Matisse, Pablo Picasso, Charles Rennie Mackintosh along with many others have been inspired by the light and views on offer here in Collioure. Inside the Restaurant /Bar Templiers which has a particularly attractive terrace on Avenue Camille Pelleton there are copies or art works adorning the walls by Picasso, Matisse, Dali and others. The restaurant had the originals left to them by these famous artists but some of these were stolen years ago and so very understandably no originals are to be seen on display today. On the quayside leading down the Avenue there are many modern day artists painting the very same scenes, some to very good effect, others perhaps are a little dubiously talented. It all makes for a lovely peaceful and atmospheric scene though.

Along the front of the small half-moon shaped beach that has the Church as its focal point there are many brightly lit cafés and most of these have a terrace spilling out right up to the beach, the clinking of glasses an ever present relaxing sound. The view from one of these tables is I feel as good as it gets and it is one that has to be savoured over a latte or a beer or a lovely chilled Rosé wine.

Many years ago Michael Palin made his first tourist film for TV and in it he finished his journey up in the west coast of Scotland and was filmed sitting having breakfast at a table by the window in his hotel. He commented that if he was to make a series of 'Greatest Breakfast Table Views of the World' then this was surely one of them. This view on Collioure beach front has to be another.

This scene gloriously spread out in front of you

does come at a premium though and if you look hard enough you can find a hidden price list for the bar just to warn you that it is one of the more expensive views in France. On a subsequent visit our daughter Charlotte did not feel the need to check this small detail but sat down with her friend in a comfortable chair ordering two small glasses of Cola. She ended up at bill payment time having to leave her friend as hostage and trawl the streets of Collioure to find me and get me to come with her to pay. Her two small glasses of cheap cola were the equivalent of over 10 English pounds, a quite extortionate sum but you are definitely paying for the view. I think she was probably expecting to pay around 2 pounds or so at most. You may feel that it is a better option merely to enjoy the view and eat or drink elsewhere later. I have a photo of her taken after we settled up with monsieur, bill in hand looking very aggrieved with her mother clearly mouthing 'You paid HOW MUCH?. A lesson expensively learned.

If you walk around to the other side of the bay you will find some more lovely restaurants and these give a view back across the harbour towards the church and beach and the little white chapel on the small hill behind the church. In some ways you may feel that this is an even better view and a little less expensive perhaps because it is quieter and you have to do a bit of walking to get there. It is a very pleasant stroll around the bay going past the Chateau Royal and on our next visit we ate on the terrace at the Restaurant Le Neptune and enjoyed a wonderful fish and seafood meal with this glorious view before us. Good memories.

On this first evening visit we soaked up the lively vibrant atmosphere with most of the cafés, restaurants and shops down the labyrinth of narrow streets staying open late. Of course as tourists we were seduced by the brightly coloured pottery so typical of Collioure and an inevitable purchase followed. Back on the seafront even though it was now quite dark there were people still on the beach just as if the sun was still out and many of them were continuing to swim out to the floating raft in the harbour that eventually held an incredible amount of bathers with many unable to stay on and overbalancing into the sea. It was an atmosphere of great relaxation and contentment and one that certainly got under our skin that evening as we have returned to this beautiful town many times over the years.

At a small bar just off the seafront we see Jacques

on his night off, straddling his Harley Davidson and holding court with friends. Clearly this coast is his 'turf' and he has many friends in the area and they appear to be enjoying a very chilled evening so we refrain from saying hello.

Sadly, this first visit was quite short and soon we had to contemplate a return by this awful mini bus back to the camp site. We actually had only been in Collioure for around three hours or so but that apparently was ample time for all the tour employees, of which for some reason there were a strangely disproportionate number on the trip, to get quite blindingly drunk. The driver fortunately was OK, well he wasn't drunk, his driving skills however were another matter. The journey going back over the winding road with occasional detours for various undisclosed reasons but all for the benefit of the tour staff was horrendous and took a nightmarishly long time. The staff just got more and more boorish on the journey and even started to brag about how much they had cheated the wine producers on our visit to the wine Chateau in Canet the previous day. They truly made us proud to be British. It was a relief to finally get back to the camp site but that evening despite the fact that it had dawned on us that the staff had actually just run the trip for a night out for themselves at our expense had for the first time shown us the beautiful Collioure and for that it was worth the endurance test.

We would return later in the week to Collioure for a full day and in future years would acquaint ourselves with the powerfully bold Collioure AOC Red wines. However the gorgeous light illuminating the bay is the star in this beautiful place but the soil and terroir and its fruits are a very close second and the wines produced are superb. We would also get to know the small village of Banyuls just down the coast with its luscious rich sweet wines, produced without adding sugar, just from what the soil bestows on them and of course with the help of that blazing sun. We would lunch well on fish, freshly prepared and with a view of the harbour to savour and eat the most exquisite desserts that we would come to expect every time from French patissiers. We would learn how to sit quietly and not to rush, taking in the views and contemplate the scene and admire the modern day artists working quietly on views that have already been painted a thousand times. And even later our daughter Charlotte would spend her honeymoon here in Collioure at the Casa

Pairal despite my best efforts to get them to miss their original flight. So you can see reasons why it is place for which we have a great affection, there are more stories to tell and we will continue to return to this beautiful part of the world, part of France but most certainly Catalan.

CARCASSONNE – CITÉ MEDIEVAL

W e had the oppor-tunity one day in that first week in France to visit the cité of Carcas-sonne. My only recollection prior to visiting this medieval heavily restored fortress cité is of having watched the English TV chef Keith Floyd exercising his culinary skills in a vineyard outside of the walls with this glorious view of the cité as a backdrop. I can't remember at all what he cooked. I always re-call that behind him you had the dazzling reflection of the bright sun reflecting on the roofs of the cité, roofs that always seemed to appear as having been just re-roofed maybe with a European Union repair grant. One unavoidable feature about Carcassonne though is that it does always divide opinion regard-ing the results of this restoration. Certainly there are many aficionados that do like their ruins to be just that - ruins. Others may lean more to wanting to see an authentic restoration taking it back to how it originally looked. These are the ones that are of the strong opinion that Walt Disney had a serious hand in Carcassonne's restoration. That can be discounted as definitely not the case as this cité was restored by the architect Eugene Viollet-Le-Duc in 1853. He also worked on the restoration of Notre Dame on the Ile de la Cité in Paris and on Mont Saint-Michel. With his plans for Carcassonne I can't help but feel he was ahead of his time, somehow having had the foresight to appreciate that one day there would be throngs of people that would have access to fast transport and this would be the time that they would flock here in droves. He also seems to have realized that one day Carcassonne would look fabulous on film. His restoration design seems to have been produced with that in mind and yes, you certainly can argue it is a bit like a theme park in places but it is surely better than being a ruin and despite all the touristy cafés and shops you are able to quietly escape the crowds and drink in the atmosphere of this incredible citadel.

Anyway all the delights of Carcassonne are for

later in the day, for our journey along the way was an interesting experience in itself. We had not travelled very far on our dreaded tour bus which today had only sober staff on it fortunately, out of Canet Plage beyond Perpignan and into the countryside. These were however hungry staff nursing hangovers and they wanted a breakfast stop quite soon after leaving the coast. The bus was winding its way down a very picturesque valley narrowing towards rocky cliffs at the meeting point of which there was a small village that looked down into the river from its square with an ancient stone bridge spanning the ravine. At the top corner of the square, a square that was probably larger than the village itself was a café. Slightly unnervingly, parked just in front of the café there are several army vehicles, the French Foreign Legion has headquarters in these parts, but I think these were regular troops. There were around thirty of us on this trip, most probably more numerous than the village population, and as we all filed in to the café for a coffee and croissant I got the distinct impression that the owner would usually only be used to serving 3 or 4 people at a time. For a small village café this could have been viewed as a cause for celebration, a whole weeks takings to be gleaned in one hour and an ideal chance to rip off the British who were still coming to terms as to how much a French Franc was worth. The lady owner stood silently behind the old bar, her face though looked far from happy, in fact it was a face that reflected the sheer terror of thinking as to how she could possibly deal with this merry crowd of tourists. The simple fact was that she couldn't and rather than immediately taking our orders it was clear that she really wanted to show us a freshly displayed closed sign and hope we would leave.

A huddle of uniformed men and women were quietly observing and comprehending the situation. It was then that the French army as represented by this small group quietly sipping their coffee, their AK-47s on the back of their chairs currently not required for use on the English, swung into action. We watched in amazement as the soldiers all moved into the cramped space behind the bar, grabbing cups and plates and laying them out on top of the bar. I think the owner wasn't aware she had that much crockery. The coffee machine went into meltdown and one of the soldiers soon returned from the village boulangerie laden with warm croissants and other pastries. I am not entirely sure if one of them stayed behind to look after the weapons while all this was going on. Within a very short period of time we were all contentedly served and the beaming owner, who had in fact done absolutely nothing to assist these volunteer sous chefs, mopped her rosé brow and counted the takings. The variety of training soldiers get these days is obviously quite remarkable and once they have finished their careers shooting people then a restaurant in Paris would surely be their pathway to riches. Great job boys and girls.

We very satisfied customers all left in a real spirit of Entente Cordial with much hand shaking and back slapping and really we could just have gone straight back home then as that was probably enough excitement for the day but on the bus went towards Carcassonne.

Whatever may be your take on the restoration of the Cité of Carcassonne you cannot possibly be other than impressed on seeing the outline of the Cité come into view for the very first time. It is magnificent and the roofs really do look extremely modern. Perhaps I expected them to be thatched. It is a very impressive sight.

That first initial impact about the architecture is diffused to some extent when you approach the main gate and pass through it into the small court-yard and then your senses are assaulted by all the Cathar themed shops in the extremely narrow street in front of you. It would appear that it is almost compulsory to be carrying a plastic sword or a cru-saders helmet while wearing a Knights Templars tee shirt emblazoned with a red cross. All the children love it but at this point I have to agree with the de-tractors that the ambiance all seems a bit contrived and somewhat like a Cathar Disneyland. On the left of the impossibly narrow street is a café that does crepes in an ancient style – you tell me. Beyond that we have a Musee du chapeau and as much as I love history I not sure that a hat museum is a big attrac-tion but it does also sell hats, presumably the ones no one wants to look at anymore. Beyond the hat mu-seum is La Taverne Medievale, in fact there seems to be one of those on both sides of the street. I assume by now that you have got the impression that this place really does try to trade on its past and that is a very violent past, one that resulted in the virtual wiping out of the culture and the resident people of this region so it seems a rather incongruous subject to now turn into mass tourism with a theme park twist. You have to smile at the beginning of the street where there is set of traffic lights that change all day long as usual, waiting to control the rush of traffic. It is quite a funny sight to see as the actual chances of even getting the tiniest Smart car up this street that is so densely packed with tourists are non-existent.

If you happen to be a history or architecture buff it is perhaps advisable to avert your eyes from street level and look up and then you are able to begin to get a feel for how this cité used to look and it is here that the restoration seems to be more sympathetic to history. Once you arrive at the top of this street after you have had your Crusader burger and Cathar Ice Cream the cité starts to open up and exploring it becomes a pleasure. It is true that once again there are souvenir shops but they become fewer and farther in between and you start to come across higher quality little shops and cafés. Flower arrangements in the streets and terraces become more abundant and there is finally space to breath. Here there are restaurants with attractive terraces and the whole place becomes extremely attractive with interest around every corner. You get an awareness of the size and strength of the ramparts and the solidity of the buildings inside the cité that once served as a protection back in the Middle Ages and earlier. Most of these walls were still fairly intact at the time of the restoration so all seems more in tune with history as you explore further into the cité.

You become so far removed from the tourist traps that you even come across a 5 star hotel, Hotel de la Cité. It is evident that here is indeed an oasis of calm and luxury within the fortifications and with us feeling slightly underdressed we simply stare inside for a brief moment and move swiftly on. Though please don't let me stop you hammering your credit cards if you are passing one day.

We as mere poor peasants from Lancashire find a crepe café and have a simple lunch of savoury and sweet crepes. The medieval theme is to be seen everywhere in this small café and you do feel you could be in real danger if one of the EBay purchased ancient artefacts were to fall down from the walls or ceiling. It is pleasant petit lunch served with a smile and you cannot ask for more than that. One bizarre thing about the meal was that the rosé wine was served in what I can only describe as glass candle holders; you know the type that only have a stem and are housed in a type of metal candelabra structure. That is how it was presented to us on the table but it did mean that practically you had to hold your glass at all times as you could not put it down on the table. All you could do was slip it back into the candle holder but then you couldn't drink could you? You would soon empty your wine glass if you forgot that it had no base to it.

It is a very hot day with cloudless skies and we are glad of these more open spaces in the interior of the cité and the taller buildings do offer some degree of shade. It is very pleasant to stroll around the labyrinth of streets and then finding once again more space and air.

In one of the lovely small shop windows was something that I really desired but I ultimately decided that because of the size of it and the distance we were from home not to buy it and for all these years since I have regretted doing so. The object was the most beautiful chess set and board with the pieces designed in what I can only describe as a very French middle ages style but the craftsman had done it in a way that did not appear tacky or cheap. The set was quite colourfully finished with all the pieces appearing to be probably painted or done in enamelled pewter. It really was calling me but on this occasion my head ruled my heart but it was wrong to do so – I should have bought it. I am now playing chess with my Granddaughter and regret it even more.

To the other extreme then, one purchase that my son did make turned out to be completely useless however and on this occasion I am not sure which part of his body told him to buy it. This was a watch and I can safely say that despite paying a considerable sum for this timepiece the watch was never worn and I think it went down the EBay route about 15 years later having resided all those years in a drawer well out of sight.

How can I describe this truly dreadful piece of design that somehow my son for at least a brief moment in time found attractive?

It was large, it was brutally metallic and angular but square at the same time. It had a little glass phial on a very tiny chain that clicked into place in a holder at the bottom of the watch face. The phial would not contain much whisky or brandy, I can only assume that it was for a powdery substance. What was he thinking? In a short space of time I think he was hoping for a refund from the Bank of Dad though he was not getting one on this occasion, he would have to live this one down for quite a while.

After all this retail therapy that turned out to be actually quite stressful, we went back through the gates to be outside the internal walls. You can walk between these and the external walls as if walking on an old dry moat. If your thing is really history and architecture then this is the part of Carcassonne that will really appeal to you. This space between the imposing walls is quite wide and you do feel pretty small as you walk around the walls taking in the detail and grandeur of this citadel fortress. The restoration seen from here seems very much in tune with the original purpose of the fortress except perhaps the roof which once again I still cannot feel is authentic to the original but despite that I have to admit it is a very fine example of the roofers art.

The finest view of Carcassonne I still feel is ultimately from a distance away from the walls and it is here that you can get a sense of the scale of the cité and appreciate with a little more empathy the planning and efforts of Viollet-le-Duc and perhaps forgive him the liberties he may have taken in restoring it in a way that maybe is not totally faithful but it does without a doubt appeal to the hordes of modern visitors.

◆ ◆ ◆

On the journey back to Canet Plage the driver pulled into Limoux, a town famous for the local wine but especially its sparking Blanquette de Limoux. This fizz is made in a similar method to Champagne and although of course they are unable to call it that, Blanquette de Limoux is just as famous in these parts as its exclusive Northern counterpart. We had some time to spare to browse the main street in Limoux and find a producer with a shop outlet that was willing to give us a tasting - a degustation. Being always happy to partake of a free wine tasting we settled down to try a few examples of this regions wine including the Blanquette. It is a sparkling wine that really is very similar to Champagne and on our future travels we would find many similar sparkling wines made outside the

Champagne region such as in the Loire Valley and in Northern Burgundy. Also for being unable to be associated directly with the Champagne name they are superb value as are genuine Champagnes from smaller lesser known Champagne producers located outside of the main centres such as Reims and Epernay. More about that in another book.

We purchased a couple of bottles of sparkling Blanquette and made our way back on to the bus. If I had known beforehand the route the driver intended to take on the way back to Canet Plage then I would have had something much stronger to drink. It would prove to be a memorable and spectacular experience though and not to have been missed. For reasons best known to himself he travelled back to Canet by the way of the Gorge de Galamus and let me tell you that precarious route is not one for the fainthearted. Spectacular though it most certainly is. When we were daring enough to look down from the window you saw that the landscape was breath-taking and somehow the driver negotiated the many rocky overhangs on the way home and with only a small wall guarding the edge of the deep ravine he managed to stay on the road and we lived to tell the tale.

France is blessed with many such gorges and this region is full of spectacular and hair raising roads. Many of them are not as well known on the tourist route as ones such as the incredible Gorges du Verdon in Provence but if you look out for hills and gorges off the beaten track you can find some amazing natural wonders that will delight and terrify you in equal measure.

It had been a great day out, a rather long one though and even the promise of another session of Jacques evening entertainment could not stir us out from our mobile home. So instead it was to be a quiet evening with a glass of chilled Blanquette de Limoux and sweet dreams all round. Tomorrow promised to be an even fuller and exciting day of new adventures and discoveries.

BARCELONA

O k, I well know that  the city of Barcelona is not in France but if Viollet-le-Duc is allowed to take liberties then so can I. Our journey did start off from France so that's my excuse for the detour in this story. Wow, this would be another country notched up by the intrepid travellers from the frozen north – so that is England, France and Spain. Must take the family to visit Scotland and Wales sometime or even Yorkshire.

Unfortunately the only words of Spanish that I knew were 'café con leche', so at least I would be able to get a drink but it was unlikely to come across that I was asking politely.

The first stop for us after a very early morning start was actually to be in Figueres for a short visit to the Salvador Dali Theatre Museum due to one of the passions of our daughter Charlotte being his extraordinary works. There is nothing at all that can prepare you for what you will find when you arrive at the Plaça Gala I Salvador Dalí in Figueres - nothing. This museum is quite unlike any that you may have visited in that the enjoyment and visual impact of the gallery starts right outside. It was Dali himself who conceived and designed this whole building and its contents after the town had asked the artist if he would leave an artwork for the benefit of the people of a community that had played such a large part in his life. So Dali being Dali he decided to bequeath a whole museum packed full of the artefacts of his imagination. The website for the museum describes the building as the world's largest surrealist object and you cannot really argue with that. Externally it is astonishing, looking like some crazy Moorish citadel with very large eggs seated on top of the battlements. Then your eye is drawn beyond that to a structure that has the appearance of a very large glass planetarium dome that you will go on to discover houses below it more of his collection. Unfortunately for us on this particular day the one basic thing that he did not design and provide is a covered shelter at the entrance and in pouring rain we had to queue for some time to get in through the ticketing area. We were all very wet by the time we had gained entrance to the museum and I suppose that went along with the surrealism of the place and there is no doubt that Dali would have been amused at seeing very wet English tourists visiting his exhibition knowing very well that for the most part we would not have a clue about what it all means.

Charlotte thinks she understands the workings of his mind.

The first space that you take in is mind blowing – a vast cathedral like space stretching up over several floors and starting the show with a large old limousine at the base of a weird tower, on the top of which is balanced a boat - what else. As you start to explore the museum you pass the most enormous canvas of a torso that appears to have an entrance to somewhere going through its middle – what was in his mind at conception was anyone's guess. There is an array of statues on high staring back down at you and the scale of the place displayed as one vast work of art is breath-taking. There are painted ceilings just as you would expect in a grand mansion or cathedral but when you look up at these the subject matter is not populated in any way with the usual angels and cherubs etc.. No, Dali wants to shock and impress and the painted ceilings that are expressions from in his mind are totally bizarre and I will not attempt to describe them. That is for you to have the joy of discovery yourself one day.

Upstairs we do find the particular trademark of Dali that so attracted the original interest of Charlotte, in fact she has a facsimile resting on her bedside cabinet that I feel sure should be giving her strange dreams every night. Of course, it is the Dali melting clock face and there are plenty of examples of this strange theme that Dali returned to develop many times in his career. In here there are also many examples of his large lips and large nose sculptures and the whole experience is one massive assault on the senses but even for a sceptic like me I have to admit that I do actually feel enriched by the surreal experience and most certainly I will never forget this visit.

We have to move on to Barcelona but only after we have had a coffee in a small café around the corner and I tried out my Spanish – I was served a glass of milk.

◆ ◆ ◆

Barcelona, visited for the first time, really what can you say? The unmistakable influence of Dali would appear to be found here also. Or could it be that it is really the other way round, is Barcelona the place where Dali first found his inspiration in the works of Antoni Gaudi. The city of Barcelona is to a large degree a monument to this one artist, Gaudi, whose architecture is to be admired everywhere in the city. His flowing architecture in the buildings that look like they have been sculpted out of the side of a cliff and displaying no two windows or entrances exactly the same are located everywhere in Barcelona and this gives this beautiful dramatic city its unique character.

Gaudi is perhaps best known for his dedicated work on the church of Sagrada Familia, his uncompleted masterpiece that totally consumed the latter part of his life. The original plans, yes there were actual plans, and building directions for his design were lost after his tragic death. He was struck by a tram on a Barcelona street in 1926 and several architects have continued the work from that time onwards without ever bringing it to a conclusion. It is scheduled for final completion in several years' time but has to be one of the longest church constructions in history and certainly one of the most costly. Milan's Duomo Cathedral does beat it for the time taken by a few hundred years even though I think the Italians always had the plans for that project. The funny thing is that when you see this Cathedral in the flesh the ubiquitous heavy cranes around the 'construction site' do almost now appear to be a part of the design and somehow do not look out of place. To stand and stare from the square opposite and take this structure in is an experience not to be missed.

◆ ◆ ◆

Another landmark in Barcelona that is not to be missed if you are a soccer fan is Barcelona Nou Camp Stadium where it would be a great thrill to see an actual game but sadly on this occasion a stadium tour must suffice. Now then, if you are not English then the next page or two may not be overly interesting to you but perhaps I can encourage you to go along for the ride and take in a bit of knowledge on a new subject for you. If not then just skip a page or two and I apologize for boring you. There is however a smattering of history in my writings as well as soccer trivia.

At the time of this our first visit to the stadium the great Lionel Messi would only be about nine years old so Barcelona had not as yet signed him to the team and the Messi 'shrine' that is part of today's museum was nowhere to be seen. For any lover of football this is the place to visit and what an interesting and comprehensive museum they have laid out here in the stadium.

To be able to understand the immense importance of FC Barcelona to the people of Catalonia you do need to go back in history to at least to the 1930's and the dramatic and tragic events surrounding the Spanish Civil War. FC Barcelona and the club president Josep Sunol made it very clear that the club was totally committed to the cause of Catalonia and the club was inseparably linked to political ideals as well as sport.

The event that to this day has underpinned the intense, bitter rivalry between the two major Spanish Clubs of Barcelona and Real Madrid, that other giant of world football, was the assassination of

Sunol by the forces of General Franco near to Madrid. Nothing could have caused a greater division between the two opposing ideologies than that and it remains a bitter memory with the people of Barcelona even now we are a long distance in time from that event in 1936.

For the duration of this turbulent period of civil war FC Barcelona mostly played out their football in Catalonia and in occasional ambassadorial tours particularly to Mexico to display their version of what in their opinion it was to be Spanish and especially Catalonian. These tours helped to put the club on the road to being the giant of world football that it is today both from a playing point of view and financially. What came out of this turbulent period was that the club became the most important focal point for an almost religious devotion to Barcelona and Catalonia, a role it has to be said the club is most happy to play and nurture. The place oozes pride and passion in its sense of place. You get another feel for the seriousness and devotion the people of Barcelona have towards their club if you visit the religious chapel that is attached to the Nou Camp. The devotees certainly feel that God is on their side and this small chapel was in fact blessed by Pope John

Paul II in 1982. It is not recorded how Real Madrid felt about that.

Our son James had brought his Blackburn Rovers shirt to the stadium, our local soccer club that we have supported over many years. He changed into it and had the ubiquitous photograph taken looking out over the pitch and the cavernous stadium. A special moment for him but probably the only time that a Blackburn shirt would be seen in this famous stadium, we might have to wait some time to see one on the pitch itself.

This visit to the Nou Camp is not just for soccer fans as I pointed out earlier. If you are a lover of architecture and engineering then there is plenty for you to admire here. This is not just in the way the stadium wraps itself around the pitch and soars up above you but from my perspective I am especially impressed with the remarkable feat of engineering carried out in 1994 of actually lowering the pitch and expanding the spectator areas at ground level. It is a truly remarkable building worthy of the legacy of Gaudi and perfectly placed and comfortably so in the fabric of Barcelona culture.

The soccer museum here at the Nou Camp is remarkable and detailed and it holds a particular fascination for us as soccer fans from Lancashire and in particular the town of Blackburn. There are important sections in the museum where the club pays tribute to former players and they don't hold back in displaying their reverence for them. Soccer players from Britain have over the years played no small part in the success of this club and it is clear from the exhibits that these foreigners are held in high esteem and affection by the Club. One of these heroes of Barcelona is the former Scottish International soccer player Steve Archibald who had a very successful short spell with FC Barcelona in the 1980's before being unable to play because of new restrictions by the soccer authorities on the use of imported foreign players. Somehow a deal was brokered and Archibald was then loaned out for a short time to our Blackburn Rovers Club in the hope that this 'star' player could take them back to the top flight of English football after many years of mediocrity in the wilderness of English football. I remember that heady time very well and it was an exciting roller coaster ride while it lasted for the people of Blackburn in having this player at the club who had recently been performing at the very highest level with arguably the greatest soccer club in the world, arriving in this small Lancashire mill town. No doubt, a massive contrast for him to find himself effectively on another planet, although being Scottish the cold weather probably did not bother him unduly.

I particularly remember one game on a bitterly cold winter's day when the local stadium was absolutely packed and Archibald showed exactly why he was a Barcelona player with a sublimely exciting performance that led to a thrillingly famous victory on the day. The crowd was so large that day and it was in the days before seating areas in stadiums were made compulsory, that I can remember going out of the stadium pressed so tightly between everyone that I was lifted off my feet and just could only resign myself to the fact that I was being carried out. It was scary at the time and not something that would be allowed to happen in these safety conscious days of today. Ultimately, Archibald despite his best efforts could not quite inspire what was a decent team to play to his higher level and the brave and exciting venture by Blackburn fell just short of its objective but Steve Archibald is held in great affection at Blackburn. He certainly is at FC Barcelona if the exhibition in the museum to his talents and time there is anything to go by.

I digress, sorry.

◆ ◆ ◆

It pays the visitor to carry on exploring around the outskirts of Barcelona and go on to visit the site of the 1992 summer Olympics at Montjuic. These games were one of the best loved Olympics of the modern era. On this elevated position the site gives you spectacular views down into Barcelona and across to the docks and coast and don't miss the sight of the long distance cable cars stretching out over the city up to the hills. The Olympic site itself when we visited in 1997 was in a somewhat neglected condition and a bit sad, a place of former glories now appearing to be without a purpose. Thankfully today it is in full use again and it is good to see that a site that produced one of the most successful Olympics has found a new life.

Of course, Barcelona is perhaps best well known for La Rambla, its most famous street. Starting at Placa Catalunya you have before you the most magical street with breath-taking sights, aromas and sounds at every turn, leading down towards the Columbus monument where you can soon gain views of the Port Vell Marina with its array of superyachts. Barcelona is a city that does have everything including a beach. For me though the best part of La Rambla is when you arrive at the famous La Boqueria market. I love food markets and can never resist going into one rather than passing by. Don't get me wrong, nowadays there are some seriously good English markets but there is nothing on the scale of La Boqueria that offers such variety back home in England. It is a major assault in an exceptional and very pleasing way on all of your senses. The scale, variety and freshness of the market produce on offer is overwhelming and you especially wish it was possible to buy some fresh fish from the extraordinary displays. On this trip it is just not practical, sadly. Perhaps a lot of this fish is obtained from English waters but as we British don't seem to want to eat anything other than cod or salmon we can hardly complain that others are more than happy to have access to such choice. La Boqueria market is just spectacular and what I particularly like about it is that it is not just a market that you merely just quickly enter with your shopping bag, purchase produce for the day and head home. No, this market is very much a social place and has this pervading atmosphere of happy conviviality with several cafés set amongst the food stalls where people are happy to meet and greet over a coffee and tapas. Once again the cafés here are decidedly male in patronage but not quite as much as in rural France. A younger mixed crowd are starting to gain control of the café culture. This is exactly the type of place you want to experience when travelling, something the like of which you can never see at home, an experience that is very new, vibrant and unforgettable.

La Ramba is throughout all of its extensive length very alive and vibrant. Alive with pickpockets also, so wallets to the front are very advisable as you stroll through the tightly packed crowds at the attractions along the centre walkway. The open spaces are teeming with street artists and in particular the incredible human statues that La Rambla is famous for. You can only stand and marvel at how these people can remain virtually immobile for hours on end, only moving when a coin is proffered to them, usually by a young child that has been encouraged to go near and then you will see the child recoil back in surprise when the 'statue' moves in grateful appreciation. It was here from these artists that I also learnt another Spanish word - 'Gracias' - and I am sure that these human statues were truly thankful that they could at last move when people make a generous gesture to them.

We made sure as we walked along that we checked out the side streets leading off La Rambla where there is more architecture to admire in the narrow streets and many enticing atmospheric and authentic tapas bars to check out. The high sided and close knit buildings have a slight air of North Africa about them, a throwback to the Moorish influence of centuries past. Like most towns and cities in France and Spain the atmosphere changes very markedly once you are away from the 'tourist' hot spots. A forceful reason indeed to take your leave and explore.

La Rambla was a place where I was impelled to try out my limited Spanish (now consisting of 4 words as you know) because Charlotte needed some antihistamines as she had a skin flare up perhaps from an insect bite that now needed attention. As the only one who could speak Spanish – really, I was unanimously nominated to be the one to go inside the chemist. Even then I only knew the shop was a chemist because of the big green cross sign outside. There then followed what is even after all this time one of the most embarrassing experiences that I ever managed to contrive on my travels. The chemist assistant apparently knew even less English than I knew of Spanish which I did think was a little surprising in view of the hundreds of tourists from Britain and the US that she must encounter on La Rambla on a daily basis. Well, if she did know any English she hid that knowledge of it very well. I somehow eventually managed to come out of the chemist shop with what I thought was the correct medication. It wasn't and I was despatched back inside for a refund and to try again. My frustration was excruciating as I was striving to get across to her what I actually wanted and losing the will to live I eventually brought Charlotte in as evidence for what medication was actually required and without a single intelligible word passing between us we did eventually succeed in our purpose. Gracias. It was so hot in the street and I was by now so stressed and sweating profusely that I really need to send another family member back in on my behalf for some calming medication.

Finally before having to leave Barcelona we arrived back at the vast Placa Catalunya and as our tired but exhilarated party was all in need of some sustenance before making the long trip back to France and Canet Plage we stepped into the Hard Rock Café. I firmly but politely told the predictably very attractive young waitress, who by the way spoke perfect English thank goodness, that we only had 30 minutes and not a second more in which to have a meal and if she couldn't achieve that then please don't take our order. She smiled at this nonsense and achieved it effortlessly and we left with grateful thanks at the end of a marvellously memorable day, a vibrant and boisterous taste of Catalonia on the Spanish side. We vowed that we had to return in the future and indeed we did.

Again, I apologize that this was not actually about France but it was a major and unforgettable part of our first French travel experience and I hope you enjoyed it and maybe if you have never been to Barcelona or Catalonia you are tempted to do so now.

LA NAVETTE – THE ONLY WAY TO TRAVEL

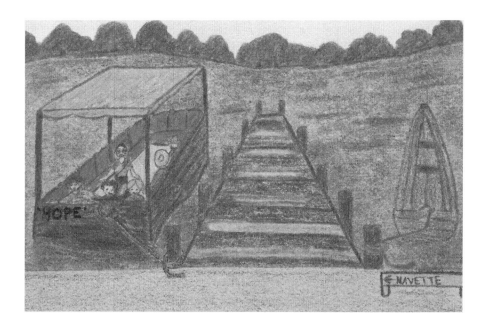

T he tiny non-ocean going vessel La Navette was an essential part of our experience in Canet Plage. As I mentioned earlier that you had in order to arrive on foot in Canet Plage town you were obligated to walk over some very unattractive scrubland to the narrow point of the stream inlet leading to the port where there was a small footbridge, usually partly blocked by local fishermen. From the bridge it was another unappealing stroll taking you past some nondescript apartments until you reached the busy marina and then on to the seafront. It has to be said that Canet in architectural terms is not the most attractive locale in the region. As a town it suffered badly during the Second World War and the town as of today is very 60's/70's in style but as a compensation it does have the most wonderful expansive sandy beach extending the whole length of the town and beyond. Also the modern spaciousness of the seafront and open squares allow plenty of scope for events to be held throughout the summer including markets both in the daytime and evening.

Many stalls on these local markets, this is true in towns and villages throughout the region, have local wines for sale and offered temptingly for tasting. These wines can often be packed in 5 litre containers as well as the usual 70cl bottles. On the markets they were very keen to offer you a bottle selection pack of three wines, red, white and rosé to wish to entice you back later in the week for more of your favourite. Buying by the container method back in 1997 would give a price costing of one English pound per litre of wine - quite remarkable. These large containers did not contain poor rough quality wines at all, particularly fine were the rosés and the reds also shone as they were strong and fruity. In these regions they could keep to producing the regulation recipe of the AOC (appellation d'origine controlee) or more interestingly they could produce a wine not subject to appellation control, perhaps using just Chardonnay, Merlot or a Cabernet grape. We also saw and enjoyed a country wine made just with the Viognier grape. Here in this region and unlike Burgundy or Bordeaux they are free to experiment and produce wines that suited them and their dry sun baked 'terroir'. Their free spirited wine producing philosophy is very much in line with their Catalonian independent character.

On these food and wine stalls a common mix of produce adopted by these local small scale producers was also to sell farm produced cheeses alongside the wines they had on offer. Sited on the market on this particular day in Canet Plage there was one such stall decorated colourfully with the vibrant cloth that reflected the Catalan love of bright colour and pattern. It looked so very attractive and enticing that we were irresistibly drawn over to it. I noticed that Charlotte was looking very closely at an object in front of the cheese display and appeared to be stroking or cuddling something. She was - all along the front of this stall by the food and wine display were several very tame pet rabbits bobbing along the length of the counter. At least I hope they were pets as they did not have a price tag on them. All I could only think of was that if you were to put on such a display on a market stall back in England it would certainly result in instant closure but here no one seemed to think this at all unusual. How could we not buy some produce after that? Later on that balmy evening in the soft pastel light back at the camp site we were very glad that we did as we sipped a chilled rosé as the evening meal cooked on the grill – fish not rabbit.

In the large central place or square in Canet Plage there is a large carousel that delights the children and there is plenty of open space around the square for them to play. Actually it is not just the young ones enjoying the communal space as you can find that you need to be very aware of the roller or inline skaters that love the wide sea front promenade. One quite elderly man, who was wearing very little, just a small seemingly home-made pair of shorts and look-ing like he was dressed for a later life Picasso look-alike competition, did very nearly run us over. Still you have to admire him for certainly not giving up on life.

The Canet night markets are particularly splendid, packed with a wide variety of traders and many characters plying their wares as well as some great tasty street food. The aromas were intoxicating and as the light fades the atmosphere becomes extremely mellow and inviting. We went over to one colourful stall that was offering food made by a young lady who hailed from Guadeloupe, her dark brown hair plaited and raised high above her head then tied in a colourful ribbon. Here we enjoyed a very tasty, spicy chicken dish from her straw covered impromptu food stall. Standing next to her was a scene of more colour in the shape of a horse drawn traveller's caravan with very colourful painted sides and rounded green roof. These people did not appear to be selling anything but were just passing through town and resting the horses just now, the beautiful light brown horse attached to the caravan was very serene and apparently napping while still standing.

Also Canet Plage benefits the visitor with a warm friendly population and you find just away from the sea front and running parallel to it is a lively street hosting many restaurants and cafés. They also have the omnipresent stalls that you always see in this particular area selling Chou Chou. These are a sweet and spicy candied peanut snack and these vendors of crunchy nuts are everywhere in the streets trying to entice you to buy a pack or two. Personally I prefer to eat nuts that have slightly less preparation thank you very much. Pizza is a favourite meal here with endless varieties available; many vendors are selling from temporary units only in situ for the summer season. The cooking smells combine to induce a desire to eat something that becomes totally inevitable so the decision is just a question of personal choice. The restaurants of the town and particularly the food stalls on the market offer food that is quite often North African in flavour alongside preparing the traditional French dishes including outlets cooking 'a la plancha'. At one such restaurant on a particularly beautiful evening we had a superb grilled meal of mixed fish, meat and vegetables followed by the most perfect crème Catalane and they also handily and thoughtfully provide hammocks for customer use at the end of your meal if you feel you are too chilled to move or have over indulged and cannot possibly find your way home.

Getting back to my description at the start of the walk into Canet Plage I mentioned the slightly tedious route you can take on foot but there is an alternative in the summer season. It is a vessel called La Navette and on all of our visits was being commandeered by a young man who sailed the short distance over the port from the Brasilia side to the marina. This a quite narrow stretch of sheltered water but still on occasions the waters could be a little choppy. La Navette was not your regular sailing vessel - most definitely not. It looked like a very flimsy temporary market stall, or perhaps more like one of those travel wardrobes with the impossibly small metal rod frame, one that could be easily dismantled and be light enough to go in the boot of a small car. The tubing on La Navette looked to be, and I am probably being generous here, around 20 mm in diameter and the intended purpose of this delicate frame was to stop you falling off and also to display advertisements for various businesses in Canet Plage including the Brasilia Camp site. La Navette had MDF bench seats that may have been from some sort of IKEA reject furniture placed all along two sides of the vessel. This contraption was all strapped to a basic raft that had improvised ballast cushions tied around it at water level. There was some sort of basic and presumably recycled engine and propulsion located somewhere below the waterline and the young man steered from a small improvised column that he stood at as Captain. It reminded me of a Boy Scouts raft race but without any Scout leaders on hand to rescue you.

The amazing business plan that clearly was very successful was that he managed to persuade so many people including us to use his boat. The fare on La Navette was very cheap but he did have lots of customers during the summer so I assume he made a decent living during the months of operation. This little raft made its hesitant way over the narrow channel as soon as no other boats leaving and entering the harbour were in view and once at the other side we delicately disembarked as the whole flimsy structure rocked gently beneath you, the smiling young man helping any that needed assistance, mainly any attractive young females. In fact it was fairly obvious that the real reason for his choice of employment was not financial success or a duty to the community but to have first look at the new batch of young female tourists and to chat them up as the week progressed. The elderly had to fend for themselves.

I have to say though that we were very grate-ful for the provision of this small rickety vessel as it saved us the long walk all the way around from Canet Plage, particularly in the dark night and it never sank while we were there. I have looked on the internet recently and it appears that La Navette has now been superseded by a smart new vessel that looks more like a flat bottomed boat and cer-tainly much safer. I was happy to see that it also has perhaps in tribute to the original La Navette a metal framed canopy, thinly constructed, very rem-iniscent of our previous transport. This larger smart vessel the website says takes 12 passengers, the old little rectangular raft I am sure took at least 24. Health and safety has finally reached the French.

THE BEACH AND THE MEDITERRANEAN SEA

Brasilia has the happy location of being right on the beach front and you can just stroll from your accommodation the short few steps straight on to the most glorious sandy beach that is undisturbed by tide, allowing you to sunbath, read or play all day long. The feature that strikes you immediately as you walk on to that beach is the intense blue of the calm Mediterranean Sea and the clarity of its waters. It is not green in the way you might expect and this apparently is because the Mediterranean has very little plankton and without plankton you get very little green in the colour. It is an absolutely gorgeous view looking out over the water to the far horizon and entertaining to speculate on where the boats that you see in the distance are heading. With some of the boats that were nearer to the shore you could even just hear their muffled conversation as if the sound was being captured in an amphitheatre requiring no speakers to enhance the acoustics. The water here laps very gently and soothingly with no hint of any drama in the tide and to quietly sit here reading and taking in the soothing sound of the sea induces a feeling of pleasant tranquillity.

Personally, I am not one to spend time sunbathing, for as demonstrated so perfectly earlier in the week I become a vibrant lobster red very quickly, so for me to be able to find a large parasol and read with just a cold beer for company is my idea of bliss. The beach is very popular however and you have to go with the flow to some extent and be happy that the children are having such a great time although at times a little noisily and high spiritedly. It is a happy place to be. With the lack of any appreciable tide and having the sand shelving gently to the sea Canet beach is a very safe place for the children to play and perhaps take an inflatable into the shallows of the sea.

Just farther down and back towards the harbour is the beach bar and all week that does a roaring trade in cold drinks and seems to be the place for the adults to gather or to meet new friends with or without the partners they brought on holiday with them. At night the beach bar becomes lively and the sounds of music drift over the camp site in an actually quite pleasant and unobtrusive way until the curfew of 10.30 pm that the site strictly adheres to. It is time for the children to sleep and in this relaxed setting with the fresh sea air the parents are not that far behind them.

Heading left to the other side of the beach from the entrance is another totally different area altogether. Again, this particular stretch of coast is quite popular with a good number on the camp site but you do not find that to be the case with many English tourists. This designated part of the beach seems to appeal more to the German tourist or ones from even farther north, from colder climates. It seemed to also appeal to many that back in their homeland indulge in plenty of food and were proud of their bodies displaying the result of their gourmet efforts. Yes, we indeed had a naturist beach just the other side of some fairly tiny signs that you can easily miss. Apparently this area is very popular for people of that persuasion, Cape d'Auge on the coast just farther north of here being a prime example of that way of life. This day I missed noting the signs and stumbled on to this part of the beach and quickly realised that it was put to such a usage. I had only managed to walk onto it for about 10 yards before the dedicated nature of this stretch of sand became apparent even to me and being from Northern England where my instinct is to put more clothes on rather than shed them I very quickly beat a hasty retreat. I never returned and always remembered to turn right on entering the beach but it would seem that for those that populated that part of the long stretch of sand that they most certainly enjoyed it as much as we more modest beach users did on our section.

◆ ◆ ◆

One early morning that week you could see many more people than usual heading towards the beach but they were not dressed in a way that made you feel that they were early sunbathers or swimmers. I dressed quickly and with James followed them down to the beach. By the sea there was the most unexpected sight of two fairly small fishing boats landed right up onto the beach and on the sand you saw that their net was bulging with the previous night's catch. These colourful boats would apparently arrive on one day every week on to this beach, usually on a Thursday and sell their fish directly to the self-catering tourists. They were a group of very happy boisterous fisherman, very pleased indeed with their nights work and the scene was quite timeless as you looked out beyond the wriggling nets and their colourful boats to the Mediterranean, an almost Biblical scene. These were men of the sea, their bodies weathered by the years of a tough outdoor working life spent supporting their families here in the south west of France. They were so clearly of the region, proud Catalans, ready to share the fruits of their lifestyle with the intruding visitors. Ideally of course, to make a modest profit also.

When I have bought fish in England it is usually from a supermarket because it was certainly the case back then in the late 90's, and in fact I am afraid that it is even more so today, local fishmongers are few and far between which for an island nation like ours is a bit of a scandal. The fish in supermarkets is always well prepared but quite often pre-packed and I find that is a bit depressing really. These very fresh fish lying on Canet beach were certainly not pre-packed. No, they were very much still alive, freshly caught but certainly not prepared for cooking. No point asking your fishmonger here. They were mainly small sea bass and dorade and after you had made your selection the fisherman would take the fish and slip them into a plastic bag and hand the lively squirming container back to you so as to return it to your accommodation. It was for you to decide the most humane way to start preparing your purchase for the pot. Our education in French ways was definitely moving on a pace that morning.

We had eaten very well so far this week, buying some excellent local produce on the Canet market and from the on-site butcher. In a setting and climate like this nothing though compares with fresh fish and our morning's beach purchase for our supper that night with a glass of chilled Roussillon rosé wine was superb. To have the pleasure to be able to eat outside on a balmy southern French evening with such wonderful fresh produce is a joy to savour and the perfect antidote to the frequent chill of a northern English summer. C'est manifique.

The beach alongside the camp site would play a large part in our enjoyment of this beautiful place in the immediate years that followed our first visit as we returned at the behest of our teenage children for 3 or 4 more memorably happy visits. On those trips there would be the fireworks of Bastille day eve, the celebrations of July 14th put on by the camp site staff with lots of wine and Sangria flowing, the incredible aerobatic displays of the red, white and blue aircraft of La Patrouille de France, performing above your head right along the beach and many more happy times to savour. These are for later and I will write of them but I would like to think this gives you a flavour of the joy to be had in this beautiful Mediterranean setting.

THE LAST DAY OF OUR FRENCH EXPEDITION

T he final full day before heading home was a sporting one, for young and old alike. The camp site staff had organized a soccer tournament that appeared to be organized along national lines as regards team selection and also a tennis competition that consisted of just a singles tournament. I had entered for the tennis tournament earlier in the week and patiently waited for a few days to see the competition draw posted up on the camp site notice board. It turned out that I had been drawn to play against a German tourist and looked forward to the chance to show my skills and progress in the competition.

Back in the day when I was in my late teens I had played a lot of tennis, probably most nights of the week and become good enough to be asked to enter county competitions although I never actually did start on the road to Wimbledon. At that time I was too busy playing cricket as well and that for me always took priority. So my confidence was high despite ignoring the small fact that I had not really played for around 20 years. I could only ponder that Germany had only produced one great male tennis player in Boris Becker so it was not likely that my opponent would cause me too much trouble.

I strolled confidently down to the tennis courts and was a little disappointed not to see a crowd forming to watch us perform. Come to think of it none of my family had come to watch me either. Perhaps they sensed that my confidence was perhaps just a little misplaced. My opponent was not at the court when I arrived and after waiting for five minutes or so I saw a slightly built gentleman walking along holding a tennis racket. I was most encouraged by what I saw in this latest moment of people watching. He was definitely not a day under 65 and I was over 20 years younger and still quite fit with all the walking we do back home and still regularly playing cricket in the summer. Round 2 of this French Wimbledon already beckons and maybe soon a trophy for the cabinet back home. Oh, how wrong I was.

The contest started well enough, as I fired a couple of good serves in and that seemed to have me on track for victory but these strokes turned out to be most of the points I ever got for the rest of this one sided German demolition job. I had misread the signals, appearances in this case were beyond deceptive and I can only assume that this guy was Boris Becker's father or coach as he was a little tennis genius who was also much fitter than me despite his advanced age. His unerring placement of the ball made me look stupid and no matter what I tried his tennis brain was purring at least two steps ahead of me. I was so relieved that there was not a crowd and I spend most of the time when I incessantly turned away to slowly retrieve the balls that whizzed past me thinking as to how I could put a favourable slant on this fiasco when I got back to the family. Believe me there were no redeeming features to this embarrassing display.

We shook hands at six-love and really I would have liked to have shaken hands much earlier. He walked away still looking all of his years, having hidden his actual prowess and fitness very well and I could see even from behind him that a German victory over the English had produced a fixed smile on his face that I assume was still there when he got back to Germany. I also assume he won the tournament but I never went back to the tennis courts to find out.

◆ ◆ ◆

So we move onto the Soccer tournament. I did not enter that although I had played in a friendly game with a few different nationalities earlier in the week and did not perform too badly but my physique is not ideally suited to soccer – cricket is my sport. My son James did enter the competition and he is a decent player although a touch over competitive but I cannot really blame him for that hereditary trait I am afraid. Years ago growing up when we brothers used to play pitch and putt golf on holiday as children I am sad to say that any sign of possible defeat could produce the throwing of golf clubs around the course in fits of despair. Sport was a serious business in the Atherton household - 'it is not the taking part that counts but the winning'.

The soccer tournament had started well in baking hot temperatures and 'our' team progressed comfortably through the first stage. Interestingly, a current member of the FC Barcelona first team was here on holiday with his young family and was playing in the tournament although he was not allowed to play in his normal position in fairness to the opponents. It was a bit of a thrill for James to play against a celebrity tourist, especially as he loved to watch Barcelona on TV back home.

As the tournament moved through to the semifinals the atmosphere changed from one of a happy gathering of multinational teams enjoying a game and friendly banter to one of deadly seriousness as national pride started to take over. The game, shall we say, got a bit physical with a good number of heavy unnecessary challenges being made by players of both sides - French and English. Inevitably after one nasty, bone crunching challenge too many it got physical in the sense that the actual football itself became irrelevant. The game was abandoned and the players were encouraged to disperse back to their accommodation rather than the bar.

Shortly afterwards the announcement came over the tannoy of the camp site: 'le tournoi a été abandonné' and it was never to be restarted. In fact because many of the players were also staying on site for the following week, they called off the tournament for that week as well. I think the tennis was once again held without incident.

So much for 'entente cordial'. Security, well Mathieu stood at the door, was a bit tight at the bar that evening although by then everyone was friends again and most participants were secretly glad it had ended early as the temperature was too oppressive and really they all just wanted a beer and chill out with each other again. We had a final night in the bar enjoying Jacques and his team encouraging many who were leaving for home on the next day to join in to be helping and taking part in the show. Diego was charging round the tables trying to sell more Mont Blanc cocktails and be able to use his cigarette lighter to set them on fire. Sylvie was still her snarling self to Diego but charm personified to everyone else as she worked the tables and took more customer orders. All was well with the world and we strolled back to our mobile home on a beautiful evening with a magnificent sunset in front of us to regrettably prepare for the journey home.

The next day I unrealistically felt that we had the time to get on the bus to Perpignan and recreate our first meal at La Malassis. We hadn't the time really but it was something we decided that we needed to do. On the crowded bus Charlotte was brazenly chatted up by a young French man who was totally unconcerned that she had protective parents and a brother either side of her. I am not sure how much of his French chat up lines Charlotte actually understood but he seemed to be pretty sure he could reach a future understanding with her by the time we all got to Perpignan and he ignored all the hard cold stares we were sending his way. The relationship did end at Perpignan and the family stayed together rather than going to the Mairie for a wedding ceremony.

Our new friend M. Argenson was very glad to see us and we explained that we had only a limited time before we simply had to get the next bus back to Canet Plage. He fed us extremely well and quickly and we said our hurried goodbyes. This dining experience was quite unlike anything I had come across in England. A restaurant visit back home was often merely a transaction, usually enjoyable but nothing more - you eat and you go home. This felt more like you were going to be leaving friends with the knowledge that you would not see them for quite some time, if ever. This was a feeling I had never felt before and a clear sign to me that France and the people we had met had got under our skin and would stay there and we would be thankful for that over the years.

◆ ◆ ◆

Back in Canet Plage after another perilous journey on La Navette as it navigated over the choppy waters of the port we quickly grabbed our suitcases and bags and stumbled up to the returning coach just about in good time for boarding it but we had taken a real chance with timings in visiting M.Argenson to say our goodbyes although it was something we simply had to do.

It had been difficult to say goodbye to the café in Perpignan and M.Argenson but it turned out to be nothing compared to the farewell scenes surrounding the departure of our coach. Look, come on, we are English and we don't show our emotions. Yes, there had been a slight flickering of suppressed feelings at the café earlier in the day but that surely is as far as it goes.

Actually No!

This trip has changed not only our travel plans but to a degree our lives and that is evident also with the reactions of many of the other first time tourists that came with us on the coach from England. This saying of goodbyes was awful and unlike anything I had gone through before. The children were in tears, real full blown tears, at saying goodbye to Diego and his staff, the tour reps who had looked after us so well but most of all from specific friends they had formed attachments to during the week, friends who were staying on for another week and in reality they knew they would probably never see again.

When we reached Montelimar the coach was still silent save from some finally wiping away the last of the tears. Things had dramatically changed for us. The next travel experience we take would again be to France and as we had now shed our English inhibitions, we actually looked forward to being able to meet other people and to moving on to exploring other areas of France. We could, we really could do this, we could be Europeans and join in rather than sit on the side-lines. We would come to Brasilia perhaps another three times, all the staff we had met from the camp site would still be there and for that couple of weeks other new friends would be made.

OUR RETURN TO CATALONIA - WHAT HAPPENED NEXT

W e did come back to Brasilia on three more occasions with our teenage children and re-produced the most fabulous of times.

All the staff we knew were still there except on the third visit Sylvie and her daughter had gone - Diego had stayed, still not ready to take the total plunge into adulthood.

The journeys down from the North of England were always taken by coach and for the most part were unremarkable and similar to the first time we had come.

Except that is for one.

In the Midlands of England our feeder coach was joined by a mother and her teenage daughter. The mother quickly and unnecessarily explained that the trip was to give her daughter the quiet environment for her to be able to study for her forthcoming exams. The general unspoken consensus was that the young lady would be best advised to become a supermodel and get her fame and fortune that way. It certainly seemed a stretch too far in the imagination that she would spend all her time reading books and revising.

The week progressed and she partied hard, fighting off the attentions of every single young man on the camp site. She was a nightly star performer on Jacques shows which did not exactly give her a low profile. Still her mother insisted that the studying was progressing well and she was such a sweet innocent child at heart. The one or two young lads that had travelled on the same coach still felt that they had a chance of pairing up with this vision.

All that ended when after a period of extensive studying she was seen coming back at breakfast time from a night spent on the sand dunes with the bookish Mathieu - Yes, Mathieu. Did she pass her exams, who knows? Mother knows best.

❖ ❖ ❖

An additional pleasure on two of our trips to Brasilia was that Charlotte was able to take a couple of different friends from home with her. One of these was a friend from college named Adele who was a petite young lady. They had a lovely inseparable time together and we very much enjoyed having her around.

One day we decided to make the coastal journey to Collioure by bus and headed into Canet Plage to find the starting point. There were only three buses along the coastline on any given day so we needed to be on time. The bus duly arrived and we formed a line as we boarded and I instructed the driver:

'Quatre allez retour pour Collioure s'il vous plais, Monsieur'

'Quatre' He puzzled.

'Oui, Monsieur, Quatre'

'Trois peut-etre? Three?' Holding up three fingers.

'Non - Quatre'

He looked down our line counted to three, glanced back again and now caught a glimpse of Adele bringing up the rear just behind Charlotte who is herself quite petite.

Rocking back in his driver's seat he laughed:

'Ah, oui, mademoiselle et tres petite' and he beamed a smile.

Adele did not.

◆ ◆ ◆

Our party all went separate ways on arrival in Collioure and we of course decided to have a long lunch on yet another hot day. We had very much got into the routine now of doing as the French do and stopping all activity for a couple of hours at lunchtime to relax and enjoy a meal.

We found a tempting restaurant down one of the cooler winding back streets of Collioure and settled down at an inside table. It was most certainly a day to accept the offer of a carafe of ice cold Sangria and naturally assuming it would be similar to Diego's somewhat watered down version back at the camp site we very soon emptied the carafe. I had also already ordered a bottle of rosé wine to go with our lunch but on a blisteringly hot day we felt more than ready for that added refreshment also.

The superb meal was slowly savoured and the rosé went down a treat and everything felt very well with the world. It was time to pay the young lady and head out into the town. It was then that I realised that I had no comprehension of where the restaurant door was or how to find my way to it. Niamh felt the same.

Strange to have a restaurant without a door.

This carafe of Sangria had apparently not been watered down and its effects were taking hold. By a process of elimination i.e. discounting the windows, we did find the door and then thankfully an unoccupied bench seat on the harbour front. All felt perfectly well with the world, it had been a great lunch but the extra Sangria left us feeling very sleepy and with no inclination to stroll the streets we dozed happily until it was time to make our hesitant way up the street to board the last bus back to Canet. Just be warned, you will not necessarily always be short changed on the quality and strength of your Sangria and it may not turn out to be of the consistency of a light soft drink. Most pleasant.

◆ ◆ ◆

A most delightful feature of Collioure and one that calls out to be savoured after a long leisurely lunch is the sight of the brightly coloured fishing boats bobbing around in the harbour. These boats represent the time when Collioure was extremely famous as a port that hosted a large anchovy fishing fleet. Over a hundred years ago Collioure would have had nearly a thousand fisherman solely dedicated to catching these intensely flavoured small fish. Only about two operations dealing with anchovies now exist here but Collioure anchovies are still much sought after. The view from the beach front by the harbour and the large blue sky with these vibrant boats in the foreground has to be one of the finest in France. Collioure is a place we treasure and now return to as often as we can.

One journey we made to Collioure by train from

Perpignan nearly ended early when I assuredly said to a puzzled Niamh that we had arrived and it was time to get off the train. She reluctantly did leave with me, going passed a bemused cyclist in the carriage who was clearly wondering why we were disembarking here. It was only when on the platform that I realised the mistake – the large unmissable signage gave it away – and rushed Niamh back onto the train, having to hold the carriage doors as they closed. It would have been a long wait for the next train and a ruined day. The cyclist found it funny.

A journey we also embarked on from Perpignan during a stay at Canet was by train to the rugged terrain surrounding the village of Villefrance le Conflent.

Villefrance le Conflent is officially designated as one of the most beautiful villages in France and has three UNESCO World heritage sites set within its boundaries. Sébastien Le Prestre de Vauban commonly referred to simply as Vauban was a famous French military engineer of the 17th Century who is considered in history to be the foremost expert on fortifications of that period. His imposing Fort Liberia that overlooks the fortified town is one of the World Heritage sites and after a steep climb it can be visited along with the ramparts of the actual town itself.

The town has many old buildings set alongside cobbled streets housing many artisans and cafés. It is a delight to stroll these ancient thoroughfares and always coming into view is the towering mountain backdrop with Fort Liberia at its heart. It is a stunning place and well worth the effort of making the journey. The prehistoric caves set into the hillside around the town also form a part of the network of fortifications that Vauban created in this mountainous region.

St. Jacques' Romanesque Church with its rich furnishings is a peaceful place as is the square surrounding it and this is a place to linger.

Villefranche-de-Conflent is also the Little Yellow Train's home starting point, this much loved train is very much a symbol of Catalonia and the regional colours that the train so proudly bears. This is a formidable technical achievement that historically linked Cerdanya's high plains to the rest of this rugged region. Today the Yellow Train is a much used tourist attraction which should be unmissable to all who come here although on our visit we ran out of time to do that precipitous circuit and it is still on our 'to do list'.

Most of the 1909 built carriages are still in service and incredibly this little train climbs up the hillside to around 5000 feet taking it close to the Spanish border - a distance of some 40 miles that defies all conventional engineering possibilities.

The station and site of the wide expanse of sidings at the departure point of 'Le Petit Train Jeune' is very atmospheric with the ancient town below you and the mountains towering around the station and the tracks. I cannot help being mentally transported back in time to the Second World War and the way these mountains were the focal point of an escape route to the Spanish border for many people, including allied airmen, fleeing the Nazis or simply using them as a base to be able to resist the occupation. It is the same imagery that comes to mind when we later toured similar parts of rural Provence. It captures a moment in history with its dramatic landscape.

On the very pleasant journey by train back to Perpignan you pass through the Commune of Prades that is home to a popular classical music festival. Prades was home to Pablo Casals, the famous cellist, and the festival is as a consequence of his connection to the Commune. He found a safe haven here after fleeing the attentions of General Franco during the Spanish Civil War.

One of the constants on our early trips to Canet Plage was to visit M. Argenson at his café in Perpignan. Always on our appearance in the doorway of his small café we were instantly recognized and greeted as special friends and this reunion was always a highlight of our trip. One day we were sat at one of the outside tables on the tiny terrace enjoying a light lunch. We were just sleepily watching the world go by between sips of chilled white wine when there was surreally played out in front of us a scene that could have come straight out of one of Peter Sellers' French themed movies. Suddenly a young guy on a noisy smoking scooter came tearing past us, spewing two stroke oil fumes onto the terrace and into my wine. He was swiftly followed by one of those small Citroen police vans with the corrugated sides that seem to feature heavily in Sellers' scripts to sort of playfully indicate the perceived incompetence of French Police to English eyes. I swear this thing rounded the curve of the street on two wheels. Off they raced down into Perpignan centre only to repeat the same chase two minutes later and then a third time. I really wished I had a movie camera with me at the time. It was so funny although I assume the Police had their reasons for wanting him. They did not come back again so either he escaped or the Citroen van exploded.

◆ ◆ ◆

The final time we returned to Perpignan on one of our family trips - this would be about seven years after our first visit - we came to Les Malassis to find the little café all shuttered up and secured. There was a small sign on the window just visible through a gap in the shutters and as my French had improved over the years I perceived that M. Argenson had died recently. We were devastated at this unexpected news. I would have placed his age at about mid to late 60's but he seemed so fit and full of life although it was clear that smoking was one of his main pleasures in life. I went to enquire after him at the chemist shop next door and they confirmed that he had indeed passed away. It was the end of an era for us, this place had filled us with the hope and confidence that we could travel more extensively. It succeeded totally in doing that and we would never forget the kindness of M. Argenson and the sheer simple joy of this humble place that had no pretentions above its station but spread an abundance of bonhomie and offered great simple food. Our landmark cafe has reopened but we have never returned. The memories are of a place in time and must stay that way.

I think that it is time now to conclude our story and my first travel book that is based on the experience of visiting our very first region of France by telling the story of our return by TGV to Perpignan as independent travellers and our thoughts on seeing it afresh some fifteen years after taking the first baby steps into foreign travel.

I will tell of our discoveries in the style of a blog or diary and hope you will enjoy it.

PERPIGNAN BY TGV – RETURN TO OUR FRENCH TRAVEL ROOTS

The piercing alarm on my phone meant that we were awake early and out of our overnight London hotel at 4am and we quickly hailed a passing black cab that conveys us by an extended circular route across to St Pancras train station. I am aware of what the driver is up to and this makes it a fairly expensive short journey but I am still tired and we are just grateful to get there anyway. It is funny how most taxi drivers seem to think you are ignorant of exactly where you are going so an extra mile here or there will not be noticed. Wrong.

The restored historic station of St Pancras has a completely different atmosphere at that early hour in the morning well before the hordes of commuters arrive and we enjoy a good stroll round seeing the station in a different light so early in the sleepy morning.

We are swiftly ushered through customs and the seemingly endless carriages of the Paris Eurostar are fully booked even at this early hour and we are soon efficiently whisked through the tunnel and arrive at the Gard Du Nord station in Paris at around breakfast time.

We feel, or should I say I feel, that we have plenty of time to spare before the departure of the TGV to Perpignan and I decide we can comfortably stroll to the Gare de Lyon for the TGV, but this certainly involves walking a little farther than needed after misreading a street sign.

The TGV train to Perpignan has not yet been allocated a platform so for the moment we decide to find the loo. Because of extensive renovation works around the Gare De Lyon these toilets turned out to be hidden well away from the main concourse in a large Portakabin and this proves to be more of an experience than we anticipated. There is a substantial queue that has formed in front of the cabin and the few cubicles are guarded by an extremely dedicated and very stern woman who looks like she would certainly use the long handled mops at her disposal in the case of any trouble. I am struggling to understand why she has to go and inspect each cubicle every time someone comes out as it is taking forever to clear the queue and we have a train to catch that we still don't know exactly where in the cavernous station it will depart from. Her mission becomes clear though as you realize that you are allowed a 'liquid' visit ONLY and she is determined in her mission to be punishing any offenders contravening that rule. Goodness knows what you are supposed to do if you have just had a dodgy curry the night before. It was far easier getting through customs than this.

The details of our Perpignan train eventually flag up on the large station board just 15mins before it is due to depart and these says it will be from Voie 17. The stretch of platforms stretched out in a line in front of us appear to be numbered A to K so where on earth is 17?

Making a policy decision I assume that the excited scores of people that are now carrying cases and heading towards the exit area back towards the toilet Portakabin do at this point know where the train is located and we follow them. It takes us over five minutes walking through a virtual building site to reach our train and then we are then faced with the staff double checking all our tickets. We get on the TGV eventually and see from our window that the platform is still thronged with people trying to get on the train and I can't help thinking that there is going to be quite a delay in the TGV getting away from the station. I misread French efficiency and the train leaves on time but how on earth they managed to do it I do not know.

To our English sensibilities travelling by the TGV is a revelation compared to using UK trains. There is plenty of space and large seats; to us it is so comfortable. Also there is an upper deck with expansive countryside views and we are fortunate indeed to have a seat here. About thirty minutes out of Paris we are offered a menu for the food and drink available on board the train and an affable man comes alongside us with a trolley and asks us what we would like. We are the only English speakers in the carriage as far as I can tell and after he has served us he will probably be hoping that is indeed the case. We ask for two cappuccinos and he gives a bit of a sigh and says he will be back in a few minutes – I have to point out that cappuccinos were on the menu.

We had just made our choice from what was stated on the menu not realising that he could only get cappuccinos for us from back at the bar area a couple of carriage lengths to the rear. The un-attended trolley is left by our seat and the rest of the people in the carriage are looking menacingly in our direction still waiting to be served. Not good. Also we have the added bonus that the aisle is completely blocked and no one can progress beyond our seats.

The nice man returns with our two cappuccinos.

I say to him 'vous ete tres gentile monsieur'. He says in English ' Yes, I am VERY gentile'. I sensibly buy a chocolate bar from his trolley to increase his profits.

This is a great way to travel and I am left wondering why we have never journeyed like this previously. As we speed our way through the French countryside the TGV journey is like slicing through the layers of a cake and the specific character of each region merges gently into one. The first stop for the train is at Valence and then we race onto Nimes. After this the journey changes, the pace slows and the TGV stops fairly regularly along the Mediterranean coast but this is a very enjoyable stretch of the line that follows the curve of the sea and then the Etangs down to Perpignan, calling at towns like Sete and Narbonne. We arrive at Perpignan relaxed and ready to enjoy our stay.

◆ ◆ ◆

We have often visited Perpignan in the past but have not returned here for several years and as we stepped off the train it is immediately obvious that in the intervening years the old train station has had a major facelift. Salvador Dali called this station the centre of the world – 'centre du monde'. Back in 1965 he painted a large canvas with Perpignan station as its subject although you would be most unlikely to recognize the station from its depiction. We feel the same way just at this moment. So much seems to have changed that I really cannot get my bearings at all and although I know that the hotel is not far from the station I seriously think of taking one of the taxis outside the exit. Eventually though, after going back inside the station I realise the planners have turned the station around as regards entrances used when coming from the centre of Perpignan and once we have got over to the other side of the concourse we are back once again on familiar ground and stroll the recognizable route to our hotel in the centre of town.

The Hotel de la Loge is located near to the beautiful ancient fast food restaurant and the receptionist gives us a friendly welcome and we discover that our room is quirky but very clean and probably quiet as it is looking out over the central courtyard. This is neither 5 star luxury or a functional modern Ibis Hotel. This hotel has its own character and proves to be an excellent choice for us especially in view if its location right in the heart of Perpignan.

After freshening up after a long journey that had that very early morning start we stroll out into the Loge square and reacquaint ourselves with the town. The big change we sense immediately is in the ambiance of the place, especially with the retail landscape. Perpignan has definitely gone upmarket with the shops in the centre being filled with designer shoes and clothes and many of the residents that are promenading that evening are dressed in a fashion that shows they are clearly not afraid of paying these prices. While I recall that the centre of Perpignan was never exactly run down or shabby in character this is a marked change in fortunes. Perhaps the reason is because of Perpignan coming more to prominence in European rugby circles since the time of our last visit, meaning the investment has been sparked because it is now drawing in lots of visitors flying in from abroad for rugby matches and long weekends.

The town is looking great on it that is for sure. Thankfully, the Catalan feel of the place is still very much intact and if anything that has been even more reinforced. They are still a proud people here, designer shoes or not.

One of the places we want to find is the little Brassiere Malassis where as we have talked about at the outset of our travels we first discovered our love of France.

We came back regularly almost as friends rather that clients until one visit the restaurant was shut up and a sign said that M. Argenson had died. We were very sad but ever grateful that he had shown us what was on offer in another culture. We found the Brasserie had remained open again and looked once again to be just as we remembered it and we were glad of that.

We eventually decide it is time to find a restaurant for the evening and settle down to eat at O Canto D'Amalia. We are shown to a table on the pedestrianised street terrace and it is a fine place to be on a lovely balmy evening. This restaurant is Portugese but has some simple fish specials on the daily menu as well as their traditional cooking.

Both of us decide on the whole Dover sole that we can see from the display will be of a good size and freshness and as per usual we select a local Roussillon rosé wine from the very pleasant young man waiting on the tables. I can't describe on paper how good this meal was. I need aroma and taste publishing. It was an incredibly fresh whole fish cooked on the bone to absolute perfection 'a point' and served with a lovely section of fresh vegetables. We are the happiest of customers when we are served fish as superb as this. We tell the waiter that they probably obtained it from 'our' fishing grounds back in the UK but said that I couldn't fault the precise cooking by the chef.

The other diners seated all around us have been a mixed group with some couples that are most definitely on a romantic date and others just quietly having a drink or a tapas, some businessmen still working on their laptops and nibbling a bit of food over an hour or two at the table. Others come and go along the peaceful street with a kiss or two for friends seated on the terrace or the restaurant owners. This is a very relaxed restaurant and local meeting place.

Oh, and what deserts they served. It had to be L'Isle Flottant for me and unusually for Niamh she really went for the comfort food with a tower of profiteroles dripping in chocolate sauce and cream. A classy Armagnac with the Expresso rounded it all off perfectly for me and what a fantastic start to the trip this was even though we were extremely tired. Strolling back the short distance to our hotel through the chilled diners and drinkers still outside the restaurants, bars and cafés makes Perpignan feel like a wonderful place to be at this moment.

Wednesday 21st September

We most certainly slept very well indeed and

went down for an early breakfast where we meet the owners of the hotel for the first time.

Monsieur attends to the breakfast room and his wife concerns herself with the kitchen duties. They are both very friendly and the breakfast consists of the usual French Continental fare but is certainly sufficient for our needs and is of good quality. One thing we notice is that he always clears the tables without using a tray and it takes him ages to do so and means plenty of miles of walking between dining room and kitchen. Should I suggest a better method? Perhaps not.

We are seated near to an Australian couple who are touring around Europe for about three months or so and we were comparing notes regarding our respective travels. I think we eventually persuaded them to go on to Provence for their next location and offered a few suggestions regarding our love of that region. Back home in Australia they were having their farm in the outback rebuilt and decided to get out of the way until the building work had been completed. To us it does seem to be a long time to be away from your home continually living out of a suitcase but they were clearly revelling in their travels. As you talk with people you discover things that you have in common and people and places you both know and the world seems to be a very small place.

They were a lovely couple and we wished them well with their travels and especially the rebuilding of their farm.

Out in the sunny Perpignan morning we decide to head through town and go to visit the Palais de Roi de Majorca and we walk up to its location about ¾ of a mile from our hotel. The route I take brings you through the older part of Perpignan and this is an interesting area and quite a contrast to the vibrant centre of town. The architecture is old, almost ancient and is residential in a way that evokes an earlier time with the streets filled with freshly washed clothes now hanging on the old metal balconies. Once you hit the outer ramparts of the Palais it is quite a long walk around them to find the entrance and we eventually get there and at this early hour seem to be the only tourists around. At the time of our visit the Palais is being extensively renovated and we decide not to do the full guided tour around the building, saving that for another visit when there will be less evidence of all this building work. Despite this distraction the panoramic views over to the Pyrenees from the ramparts are superb and the exterior and courtyard are worth the walk up here. The Palais has incredibly thick defensive walls especially on the atmospheric tunnelled entrance staircase. Impressive. Quite a few tourists are beginning to arrive now and a couple of coaches laden with German tourists pull in to the car park below the ramparts and we decide to head back to town going by a different route that turns out to be much shorter as Niamh is keen to point out.

The town is buzzing with a lively atmosphere now and we find that a busy market is taking place in the large square that previously used to have an indoor market hall but that structure has now been demolished to open up the square for restaurant and café tables and this new outdoor market. The square looks much better laid out this way. Once again this vibrant area with the market and fishmongers really makes you wish that you were self-catering. We vow to do that on some other visit, but as is so often the case our immediate response to sights like this in France is that we do feel very jealous that people have such an abundance of quality fresh produce like this readily available to them on a daily basis. Why can't we have this back home? Maybe the sunshine helps but more likely the supermarket domination and a lack of imagination causes the un-imaginative situation back home.

We continue to browse the shops for a little while and they are a joy to look round but not always affordable. Again I can harp on about the differ-ence to the UK where we have so many uniformly boring high streets and supermarkets. Perpignan is like most larger towns in France in that it has inde-pendent shops offering a wide variety of interesting choices and price points.

There must be twenty shoes shops alone in the centre of Perpignan. Thinking of the town back home where I work, we are not talking about a small town here, there are no shoe shops at all in the town centre. It is safe to say that Niamh is enjoying this browsing of excitingly different shops very much indeed. We inevitably look at the jewellers shops as some years ago Niamh chose some beautiful garnet jewellery which Perpignan is famous for. I think having viewed them again on this occasion we can be happy that at the prices we paid back then they were also an excellent investment. There was one other shop that we especially wanted to find and that was also a jewellers where we had purchased some Lalique glass jewellery for Niamh on our first visit many years ago. It sadly was closed and actually up for sale, although all the stock was still in its place in the window. It has the appearance of a circumstance of where the proprietor had probably died very recently and the shop had just been left as it was. We could see the Lalique range in the shop window and he had also been having a sale on as well but a purchase although tantalizingly close was not to be this time around.

We decide as we often do in France that it is lunch time and we go back to the open market square to choose a restaurant. We decide on Restaurant Delmar in the square which has a good fixed lunch menu and lots of tables under cool shade alongside the market and these tables are occupied by locals which is something I always look for.

Niamh orders a Nicois salad and I am tempted by the plat de jour which is an entrecote steak served with boulangere potatoes. Both are excellent but we decide against having a desert as we would prefer to leave room to enable us to eat out again in the evening. The service was good and a chilled jug of Sangria with our meal made this a most enjoyable lunch stop.

By this time due to my extensive walking tour Niamh is having problems with her shoes and really needs to find another more comfortable pair and I suspect that with all the shoes shops here in Perpignan this should not turn out to be that much of a problem. We soon realise that the only drawback is that it is clear that they are nearly all designer shops and not offering the comfort she needs - or the price point I need come to think of it. Eventually, and it is eventually, we stumble on a shoe shop on the quay by the river canal. This is a Chinese owned shop that is very similar to one we found in Paris the last time Niamh had a major shoe emergency. They have lots of choice all at amazing prices and a pair of light comfortable shoes is easily selected.

They will in the coming week take Niamh all around Paris as well, so not at all bad value for 10 euros.

Outside this shop on the quay is a book market, stalls I always find to be quite irresistible, and we have a good browse through, being tempted to buy a couple of times but I really don't want to add to the weight of the luggage which is the one drawback of touring by train. Perpignan does looks absolutely superb today with clear deep blue skies setting off the plentiful variety of flowers in the vivid displays all along the two quays. The clear light today really shows off the Castelet and other buildings around it with their distinctive Catalan colours. With plenty of Catalan flags on view the scene is a very colourful one and we sit on the quay for a while enjoying the views and the ambiance.

It is time for a siesta and the hope that we will be ready to eat out again by the time evening comes.

More food. Really!

That evening we find it is difficult to choose a restaurant, we are a little spoilt for choice here in the centre of town and you can start to overthink it sometimes when this is the case, always looking for that something just ever so slightly better.

We find ourselves back in the Cathedral square in front of the appropriately named restaurant Le Saint Jean. This has a very quirky window frontage emblazoned with its French restaurant caricatures, very 'Allo 'Allo (again apologies if you are not English, and even greater apologies if you are French.)

The restaurant has a shady courtyard set out with tables right next to the high Cathedral wall and it just feels like the place to be tonight. The very pleasant young waitress leads us to a table.

We start our evening dining with a local rosé and order our food, Niamh again has a salad and I select the fresh sea bream. It is all rather excellent although I think Niamh wished for a slightly less generous portion having had a good lunch earlier. The courtyard slowly fills up as people stroll past, look at the menu and think the courtyard is as inviting as we did, but Perpignan is so laid back that diners seem to just want to stroll for a while and take their time, eating late here is probably very much the norm.

Now, back to the food and the star of the show tonight is undoubtedly my dessert.

It is one of those plates that you see quite regularly in France now, La Assiette avec une Café. It has become a trend that a good number of restaurants seem to offer this as a feature dessert, building a series of small desserts around your final café of the meal. This plate is a fabulous six part delight. It was a lovely meal in an unusual but interesting setting and we had excellent service. The young lady missed putting the charge for the wine on our bill but the quality and value of the meal certainly did not deserve them to be short changed so I told her of the omission and she was very grateful. A most enjoyable evening and we strolled back past the ubiquitous noisy Irish Pub to our hotel on a clear balmy night.

Thursday 22nd September

We are up early and after breakfast we head for the train station, Salvador Dali's 'centre du monde'. We are taking ourselves off to journey down the coast to Collioure and we are pleased that the train arrives on time as we are so looking forward to this trip as Collioure is one of our very favourite places and it feels as if it has been a long time since our last visit.

The train is quiet and having never been to Collioure by train before I decide that as it pulls into a station at the designated time of arrival we should get off. I hadn't realized the train was three minutes late but Niamh had and with some reluctance she followed me from the train. On the platform and with the train primed to leave I realize there is actually another stop and we are in Argeles Plage. I dash to the door and have to hold it as Niamh dives back on and we fortunately just avoid wasting at least two hours waiting for the next train. That was close and nearly very embarrassing, well even more embarrassing really.

The narrow streets from the train station wind gently down to the harbour and we soon have our first view of the fishing village we love. It seems little changed, of course there are new shops and restaurants but essentially the character of Collioure is quite the same as we remembered. It is so wonderful to be here again just strolling around and taking in the fabulous views on what is a perfect day with a cloudless sky and the temperature already very warm.

The local artists are out early and in force on the harbour, painting for no doubt the thousandth time the timeless view of the port and the Eglise Notre Dame des Anges. The harbour has many cafés with parasol shaded tables going right up to the beach and lots of people are already enjoying a coffee at the inevitably inflated prices. You will recall that we have often said that if someone decides to do a compilation of 'great views from a café table' then this has to be right up there with any other suggestion in the world.

Walking around the back of the Eglise we go over the narrow causeway and up to the tiny white Chapel on top of the headland, the route taking us past a new brasserie situated right in front of the beach. From the chapel you are able to walk across the top of the harbour sea defences and get a fabulous view back to the village and it does looks stunning today in the incredible light that is a feature here and this radiance has drawn (sorry) artists to Collioure for decades. Of course I take lots of photographs but really try hard not to include the iconic Eglise too often but it is difficult as it is such a feature of the village landscape.

We walk back past the chapel and browse the many shops located through the narrow streets and here we find a welcome shady coolness away from the bakingly hot beach front. Niamh decides on a gentle and non-too deep paddle in the shimmering bay and for me it is a very welcoming break just to sit on the stone steps and chill out in front of the Chateau by the harbour, exchanging smiles with people as they past or sit nearby. Collioure is in some ways a village split in two with another beach and bay that can be enjoyed by going around the side of the chateau taking you away from the village and it is to there we decide to stroll and look for our lunch table. Compared to other villages along the coast it is fair to say that there is a premium on the prices displayed here, purely because you have this impossibly beautiful view arrayed before you looking back to the port and village. It is however a touch cheaper generally than at restaurants on the beachfront by the church. We rule a couple of restaurants out as just ridiculously expensive and go back to the first restaurant that we had previously also ruled out despite the owner pleasantly offering us a card when we passed by. This time though we notice they do have a couple of fixed price menus that if we factor in the extra premium for the gorgeous view makes it just about a sensible option.

The tables are located on a raised terrace and the striped parasols pleasingly shelter you from the fierce sun. The view is superb and really does it get much better than this? – Lunch on a glorious day on a shaded terrace looking back over to Collioure harbour. Service is as usual carried out in the southern French laid back style but efficiently done and who wants to be rushed here anyway when you are paying for this view. In this gorgeous setting with the lapping sea in front of you it just has to be a choice of seafood today and despite the heat I just have to have the soup de poisons with rouille and croutons. It is so good and I vow to attempt to recreate this in coming English winter which I do to the delight of our friends back home in Lancashire. As good as my cooking was it is I have to say a somewhat more fulfilling experience to eat such a dish in the heat and setting of Collioure harbour. We both have the pan fried salmon (Scottish) and this is sublime and with the inevitable crème catalan to finish all washed down with a bottle of the local rosé we are more than happy. What a lunch. The only negative aspect of the meal was Niamh's dessert which was highly unusual in being one of those things you see on a menu and instinctively think - 'that's interesting', but in the end turns out to be EXACTLY what it said it was. Strawberry milk shake with fruit turned out to be just that with not an imaginative twist in sight and as the kiwi fruit tasted subtly of garlic it rather flattened the finish of the meal for Niamh. Nevertheless she was not getting any of my sublime Crème Catalan.

An essential siesta on a stone seat by the harbour was most certainly needed before we headed back to the hotel and after a little more browsing of the shops in the narrow shady streets and then watching the French marines exercising in the bay (in this heat) we sadly took the train back to Perpignan.

Finally, for once we did find that evening that we were really not very hungry and so grateful that the waiters at the bistro in the Loge square indulged us by allowing us to occupy a table for a couple of hours over a coffee, beer and Banyuls wine and soaking in the ambiance on a wonderfully balmy evening. We slept well.

Friday 23ʳᵈ September

On this trip we are scheduled to move on to Paris for a few days and after a last morning stroll around Perpignan we head for the train station purchasing a lovingly wrapped fougasse from an impossibly beautiful display at a boulangerie along the way, this to serve as lunch on the journey on the TGV.

On the station information display the train is unfortunately shown to be scheduled for a delay of thirty minutes and we really did not want that. It is so very hot on the platform with very little shade but fortunately the expected delay is reduced and we ultimately leave Perpignan station around fifteen minutes late. As the train heads out from Perpignan it soon becomes clear that the air conditioning in the carriage is not working and the air becomes very quickly incredibly hot and is really getting unbearable. I make several trips to the toilet to soak a cloth in cold water for Niamh so that she can try to cool down a little. The very smartly dressed young TGV lady comes round with cold water for everyone but she says that they can do nothing to rectify the situation as yet. At Perpignan station we had noticed another TGV official getting on the train and he was middle aged, overweight and unusually had very long and thinning hair, not the usual corporate look. He also came around the carriage and spoke to passengers and we struggled not to smile as he explained that as soon as the TGV arrived at Nimes they would move us to another carriage. The amusing thing for our silly English sense of humour was that he looked uncannily like Peter Sellers in that Pink Panther film when he is dressed up as the long haired mad doctor with the false nose that slowly melts down his face in the heat. This guy who was perspiring for France looked just like that (although his nose didn't melt) and if there was anyone who needed a cooler place to be it was him.

It turned out well though as we ended up on the upper deck giving us the great view of the French regions as we sped north and the story continues in Paris and I will return with my memories of that city in another book.

WHERE TO NEXT ON OUR FRENCH TRAVELS

O nce the children came out of their teenage years Niamh and I branched out on our own travels to France. We took our car over the channel, by ferry or the Eurotunnel, we went on organized wine tours, we also visited vineyards ourselves and tasted and bought wines, we discovered Provence, we took the Eurostar from London to Paris many times and as you have just read we travelled the TGV to Perpignan. There were visits to Normandy and Brittany. In Burgundy we discovered heady fruity wines and a superb cuisine. Above all we meet some exceptional people of character and had experiences that were joyful, sad, exhilarating, sublime, crazy and unexpected. We had these wonderful times together and sometimes we would be taking friends with us or even journey on an organized group tour.

Our adventure still continues and I hope you will stay with us.

◆ ◆ ◆

To sum up our very first journey that I hope you have enjoyed I can do no better that this:

On the coach journey home we stopped at Montelimar to be joined by the coach that had gone to Spain, you know the one that fuelled the journey with beer. The men still wore the same football shirts and shorts as a uniform that they had displayed when we left them ten days earlier.

A young woman came out of the services shouting loudly across the car park to anyone who would listen:

'Stupid French *****, they won't take English money'

No love, they don't take French francs at your local convenience store either.

Actually I thought that, I didn't say it.

Yes, we would come to France again and we would embrace it and this incident reminded me that whatever we do here in the future we would always treat people with respect and how well that would repay us over the years in Provence, Burgundy, Loire Valley, Normandy, Brittany, Paris and of course back here in Languedoc-Roussillon and the Lot.

If you have enjoyed my book

PLEASE LEAVE A REVIEW ON AMAZON

I would very much appreciate your feedback

Many thanks   Neal

**PLEASE NOTE AS THE PURCHASER YOU CAN DOWNLOAD
THE BOOK FREE OF CHARGE FOR YOUR KINDLE**

If you have enjoyed this book I would be very grateful if you could leave a review on Amazon - Merci

Thank you for reading and I would love your feedback on my writing and can be contacted via my website : www.nealatherton.com

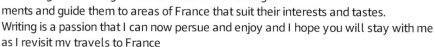

This book is the first in a series of four about our travels in France.
The next three are : PROVENCE - PARIS - WINE

I have travelled extensively in France over many years as a family, as a group and individually. I have used that knowledge in assisting others to make travel arrangements and guide them to areas of France that suit their interests and tastes.
Writing is a passion that I can now persue and enjoy and I hope you will stay with me as I revisit my travels to France

I am based in Somerset, England but I was born in Blackburn, Lancashire where I developed a love of Cricket, soccer, golf and walking. My French travels have inspired a love of cooking and sourcing local ingredients.

I have also written about Ancesty and Genealogy - A Military Story

NOW on Amazon:

My Second & Third books in this series are now available on

AMAZON

Manufactured by Amazon.ca
Bolton, ON

10824403R00139